Jack Lambert
Tough As Steel
by Ron "Tank" Rotunno

...Arguably America's best Middle-linebacker ever!

Photos courtesy of
Kent State University

Thanks to Country Lane Graphics
and Donald Pratt for their
input into putting this book together.

© 1997 Ron Rotunno
ISBN 0-936369-54-X
Library of Congress Catalog Card Number 97-92180
Steel Valley Books
764 S. Stateline Rd.
Masury, OH 44438

Ohio • Pennsylvania
Printed in the U.S.A.

DEDICATION

*To The Pittsburgh Steeler teams who, along with
Jack Lambert, stole the hearts of the Pittsburgh fans by
winning four Super Bowls.*

Acknowledgments

Special thanks go to Martha Eckman and Phil O'Connor, for their expert advice on writing this book, and to Louise Harper for her kindness and insight into the people and history of Mantua. Three sportswriters were especially helpful in providing details, locating important reference information, and making copies of their football articles: Harry DeVault of the <u>Record-Courier</u> (Ravenna-Kent, Ohio), Chuck Heaton of The Cleveland <u>Plain Dealer</u>, and Steve Hubbard of the <u>Pittsburgh Press</u> (now the <u>Pittsburgh Post-Gazette</u>).

The book wouldn't have been possible without the help of research-education assistants Pete Fierle and Sandy Self of the Pro Football Hall of Fame library. Personal thanks go to my friend Jimmy "Pine" Miller for making available his collection of sports magazines, football encyclopedias, and almanacs. They gave me detailed information needed for the manuscript. I'd like to thank John Pennell especially, Lambert's friend since childhood, for giving his time and personal knowledge of long-past events. Last, many thanks to the Kent State University Sports Information Department for a great deal of football research data — and to the Kent State University Library and the Kent City Free Library for research assistance.

To thank John "Cappy" Caparanis, radio sports broadcaster for AM WBBW/WRTK stations, Youngstown, OH, for his expert knowledge about Pittsburgh Steeler football.

And special thanks to the following journalists who encouraged me to write the Lambert story:

• Dan Saevig, director/publisher of <u>The University of ⊤</u> <u>ledo Alumni Magazine.</u>

- Editor Clifton P. Boutelle and Managing Editor Dennis F. Bova of <u>ATBG</u> (Bowling Green State University (O.) Alumni Magazine).
- Lynn Saternow, sports editor for <u>The Herald</u>, Sharon, PA.
- Donna Boen, editor of <u>Miamian</u> (Miami (O.) University Alumni Magazine) who understands the grind: "A writer is someone for whom writing is more difficult than it is for other people," Boen says this is one of her favorite quotes.
- Ray Swanson, sportswriter for <u>The Vindicator</u>, Youngstown, OH.
- Bob Carroll of the *Professional Football Research Association*, North Huntington, PA.
- The bottom line is for Lou Rotunno of Sharon, PA, who has followed the Pittsburgh Steelers since the 1950's.

PREFACE

A famous critic once said, "We can't ever find fault with anybody for not writing what he didn't start to write in the first place. All we can do is let him pick what he wants to write about and then evaluate how well he did it." Readers will decide about that by the time they finish this book. Why should a story of Jack Lambert be worth writing or reading in the first place?

Lambert achieved a towering record in the world of professional sports. His name became synonymous with the term "middle-linebacker." He's one of the best (arguably the best) who ever played the position. It's worth more than a superficial browse through some newsclippings to learn how and when he achieved his record. More important, both his fans and football aficionados have always wanted to know more about him: his character, his beliefs, whatever insights they can gain from knowing what drives a great athlete.

When a celebrity dies, all we have to understand him with are the written records. If we're lucky, we can find some people still living who knew the celebrity and are willing to share their memories of him. That's just about all I've had to work with in this book: records of Lambert's interviews with sports journalists—and interviews with the few people who know or knew him and were willing to sit down and share their memories. Jack Lambert, though very much alive, is a very "private" individual, and he has refused to return phone calls or answer letters of inquiry.

As a result, I've had to start from scratch, talking with people he went to school with, ex-teammates, coaches, and the few family members who would talk about the past. All the memories were remarkably alike, and you will find certain descriptions of Lambert occurring over and over—from the years when he was a little boy until the day he was inducted into the Pro Football Hall of Fame. You'll have to draw your own conclusions about the kind of person he is, what he believes, and how he managed to achieve his stature in the world of sports. This book makes no claim to be a big <u>exposé</u> of Jack Lambert's life: it's not a "let's bash Lambert."

This story is an effort (1) to create a chronology of Lambert's life and career in football, and (2) to condense the sometimes contradictory impressions into a coherent and, if possible, authentic picture. Knowing that sportswriters work under time limitations—and that they have to shift and shade ball game impressions to interest readers—I realize some of the newspaper materials may contain exaggerations. The "Mean Smilin' Jack" image, as an example: Lambert always objected to that description. Personal memories of ex-teammates or family may or may not always be precise, especially those from childhood, depending on the character and insights of the friend or family member doing the remembering.

TABLE OF CONTENTS

CHAPTER 1
GROWING UP

How does a kid grow up to be a pro powerhouse known as "Mean Smiling Jack" - a man whose image on the front cover of this book is imprinted in the minds of millions of football fans across the nation?

Answers to that question sent me scurrying to Mantua, Ohio, a place which wouldn't necessarily make you think of "Football Town, U.S.A." like other cities or towns. Farm country, small churches, and traditional life-styles, the Cuyahoga River (after it was cleaned up) runs downstream through the county. Mantua lies about 30 miles southeast of Cleveland, and its 1,128 inhabitants enjoy a conservative lifestyle. Many are older, retirees. Potato farming accounts for a lot, if not most, of Mantua's industry.

It's claim to fame is Jack Lambert. Lots of the folks he grew up with are still there—kids he played and went to school with; teachers, and coaches who remember him when he was a little guy. During his teen years at Crestwood High School he also attended church and church camp regularly, going to Camp Christian in Magnetic Springs, Ohio, during the summers.

I've admired Jack Lambert for years. Like other fans I've wanted to know him better. Without his cooperation I've had to do (occasionally) what we all do: <u>create</u> our own heroes in our own minds. While collecting data for this book, I was surprised when a number of people who know him well refused to be interviewed. I respect Jack Lambert's privacy, too, but I'm convinced that he deserves an accurate and fair story, <u>during his</u>

own lifetime. This book is as accurate and fair as I can make it. If it suggests some events without iron-clad documentation, it will be because, lacking Jack's personal input, I've had to create my own hero.

Jack's grandfather on his mother's side of the family was C.H. Harper. Although he died some time ago, most of Mantua still remembers him fondly and speaks of him as "Bus." Friendly and talkative, he was well-liked by most everyone. He and his wife, Elizabeth (Liz), had two children—a son, Dan, and a daughter, Joyce.

John Harold (Jack) Lambert was born July 8, 1952. The whole Lambert family went to the Mantua Center Christian (Disciples) Church then since his mother was an active member. Apparently both his parents encouraged Jack in sports, maybe his mother a bit more than his father, because he was with her more.

At that time Jack's mother was working at the Portage County Court House in Ravenna, and no day-care or pre-school facilities were available.

"Jack had a rough life as a child," said Louise Harper, a family member. "His mother worked and had to leave him with different baby-sitters."

Meeting Louise Harper was a heart-warming experience, especially after bumping into so many people who refused to talk about Jack Lambert. After I knocked at the side entrance of her home, she opened the door with, "Hello," in a fairly deep, raspy voice. Once I'd introduced myself, she said, "Come on in and sit down," and we both took seats at the kitchen table of the old farmhouse. The table was partially covered with reading materials, notepads, and some ink pens. On that windy, snowy day in Northeast Ohio and with the oncoming storm conditions it felt good to be inside. The warm and comfortable house made me relax and feel tranquil.

Then 77, Louise Harper still stood tall. Even with graying hair, she didn't show her age. She offered me a notepad and a pen to scribble notes with as she shared thoughts about Jack. She spoke slowly but to the point, obviously trying to be honest and fair in all her statements.

Louise said she came from the "old school," believing in traditional family values and a conservative lifestyle. She came across as being both tolerant of different viewpoints and an astute judge of human behavior. I knew she spoke the truth and expected me to return the favor. She seemed eager for conversation.

The inside of the farmhouse was well kept. The floor was laid with white-vinyl and the kitchen had a clean set of wooden cabinets. Newly painted walls made the place sparkle, and the old wood trim looked as if it had just been installed.

Louise took care of Jack off and on from age four through high school. "Jack wasn't a discipline problem," recalled Louise. "He was a normal kid who was just a little mischievous at times. Sometimes there was a little trouble between Jack and his playmates, John and Ray Harper. They spent time on the farm, too, and they were a little jealous of each other from time to time." Looking out the window I could almost hear them... grubby little boys out in the back yard...

"Hey, it's my turn, you were out of bounds!"

"Was not... I was in all the time."

"No you weren't... and it's my ball. Give me the ball..."

"You're not big enough to take it..."

"I am, too..." followed with the sounds of scuffling.

"Then somehow Jack never got the idea of 'doing things back' — I mean he would take things or accept things, like favors or gifts, but he never seemed to want to do nice things in return. It was nothing to get excited about. Just kid stuff." Maybe so.

As early as age four, Jack was competent in the little tasks kids learn to start off the day—tying shoes, buttoning shirts, closing zippers. At that age Jack had a leaning toward achievement — the early stages of what the experts call "developing a self-concept." He impressed his teachers and playmates as being assured and positive about the world around him, wanting to prove he could do...whatever.

"Here, let me do it...I can do it."

"Are you sure you're big enough?"

"Sure I'm sure...watch me. Hey! Watch me..."

Even at age four, he released a lot of energy in sports: an ideal place for little kids to prove their adequacy and start achieving their goals.

All of us like to feel competent at things — something, anything — especially when we're little. Later we aim for higher goals, new challenges — in school, our careers, marriages, or lifestyles. Lambert, of course, wanted the same things — he just wanted more of them: not just competence. He strove for excellence.

"Jack was aggressive when he was real young — four, five, or six years old," Jack's Uncle Dan Harper had said earlier. "He had a big need to achieve something. We weren't quite sure what. He played a lot of backyard games, and I could see how Jack went all-out. Even back then he had a need to do better than the rest."

Dan Harper is noted for one-word comments and one-liners. When asking questions, you needed to "prime the pump" with suggestions before Uncle Dan volunteered details. He never got excited when talking about his nephew.

You've known guys like him all your life. Bald and wearing glasses, he stood 5'10", about 190 lbs. Worked at home in a work shirt and bib overalls. His friends said his trademarks were a slug of chewing tobacco, an occasional cigarette, plus shooting down a night cap. "As he grew older, Lambert's mama...my sister...tried to calm Jack down, especially when he got into high school sports about age 14," Uncle Dan remembered. "He was so very aggressive and intense. I know she talked with him about 'over-doing' it." After my thanks for his interview, Uncle Dan wrapped up our session with, "You bet!" One-liner.

"Yes, Jack did have a temper and it got him into trouble more than once," Louise Harper recalled that cold wintry day. "He wanted to be the best at everything and <u>ahead</u> of everybody else. Even when playing in the backyard, him being so competitive made his temper flare up and sometimes he'd provoke fights with the other kids who were playing. And if his team lost, he was so <u>disgusted</u> with himself, knowing he and the team could have played better."

Yet Jack's need to achieve was more powerful than his need to listen to his mother and "calm down." Lambert's desire to attain new goals grew stronger as the years went by; the rewards, the positive feedback he got and the encouragement stimulated him toward aggressive behavior. Aggression? Achievement? They were all part of his home life, life of the community, and a big segment of what they call team "interaction" in sports. More than that, as a youngster he learned he would have to sacrifice to reach a goal with a high price tag, even at the expense of physical sacrifice.

Child psychologists tell us that competence is something everybody gains: certain levels at certain ages. They claim that <u>achievement</u> is a "learned action." Everybody has had those feelings of wanting to be <u>competent</u>. As we grow older, our thoughts shift to doing <u>better</u>. Being just competent will no longer hold top priority. These days we know how children begin to see the consequences of their actions; and the idea that consequences (feedback) motivate children to generate <u>more responses</u> is well supported by research.

We all respond to positive feedback, that's human nature. It builds the ego. We feel pleased with ourselves. Yet some individuals seem to <u>need to reach out</u>, to attain higher and higher goals. In sports, Lambert was one of those who needed to climb higher and higher, causing him to strive to become <u>"Tough As Steel."</u>

After a while, the kid who sets higher and higher goals for himself is working for more than simple "feedback." He's trying to earn <u>rewards</u>. He starts evaluating what he does against some internal standard of excellence. What people need to address are questions like these: "Does one <u>want</u> high achievement motivation in a child and if so, how much? No one has researched varying degrees of achievement motivation, or whether high achievement-oriented children are happy children, or nice to have around the house."

WHAT SCHOOLMATES REMEMBER

On another winter's day in '92, I stopped at Streetsboro High School before school let out for Christmas vacation. In early afternoon the temperature was down in the low 40's. All the heavy snow had melted from the previous week's storm, but the sky was overcast with a light drizzle. The cold air cut like a razor.

Walking into the school's main office, Larry Marek greeted me, introducing himself and offering a warm handshake.

"You got me at a bad time," he said. He did look a little frazzled. He sounded like what he was: a schoolteacher and a very successful wrestling coach. Somber faced that afternoon, he never cracked a smile. Marek gave the impression of a man always in a serious frame of mind, taking things in stride, but operating on a tight schedule. "We have some events going on this evening, so I'm short on time."

Uncle Larry Marek is only a few years older than Jack, and they used to oppose each other in sandlot or backyard games. One of their favorites as youngsters was dodge ball (or "war games"). As kids they often played inside the big barn on Bus Harper's farm where they worked in the summers. As young farmhands, Lambert and Marek learned about old-fashioned hard work and dedication.

"But by age 10, Jack really hated to lose. He would even climb through or on top of the hay mows — 30' to 40' high —to avoid being hit by the ball. Once you were hit, you were out. It was dangerous climbing on those mows," Uncle Larry recalled. "You could get hurt easily if you fell off."

The way he told it, I could see them... *"Hey, watch out! We're not supposed to climb up there!"* And dusty laughter from high up, *"You can't hit me up here...you can't hit me now!"*

"Come back down from there...it's dangerous up there!" "No way! You can't hit me up here..."

That risk-taking behavior pattern, according to Marek, stayed with Jack throughout his football career. Playing in games with injuries, for example.

"Jack was a skinny little runt, very competitive, lots of guts. He was serious-minded for a kid his age. He wasn't real happy-go-lucky. Seemed like he was more mature than other kids between ages 10-12. You could joke with Jack to a point. But if you pushed it too far—you got trouble... or maybe a fight"

"Whatcha mean 'skinny runt,' anyway? Size has nuthin' to do with whether you're good or not!

"Maybe you guys got some inches on me, but you'll never take me for granted...!"

We walked out into the hallway together. "If I can be of any more help, you know where to find me." Larry Marek and I went our separate ways, thumbs up for good luck.

EARLY SIGNALS OF TALENT

Jack's father, John H. Lambert, was also a good athlete. "Old Jack" was an outstanding football and baseball player at Shalersville Local School, down the road from Mantua. He was on their six-man football team. Later on, Lambert, Sr. played third base for Samuel Moore & Company's employee softball-team in Mantua. An achiever in his own right, Jack's dad played <u>intensely</u> whatever team he was on, so young Jack Lambert came by his intensity honestly.

At that time the Cleveland Browns were Jack's favorite pro team. During breaks in his farm work, Jack used to visit the Browns' training camp at nearby Hiram College where he collected autographs from notables like Jim Brown. A lot of Lambert's friends took the ride with him down scenic route #82 into Hiram. All the kids were caught up in Browns' mania.

Jack's mom began working for Samuel Moore and Co. in 1969-70, too, as a secretary for the sales department. She enjoyed sports, was something of an athlete herself, and became a member of the company bowling team. She and Penny Bishop bowled on the same team at the Sky Lane in Garrettsville, Ohio. "Joyce was a good bowler for us, too," Bishop told me. "She helped our team a lot."

At age eight, Jack joined a Little League baseball team at Mantua Center Christian Church. After an announcement at the church one day, Lambert signed on to play in the Mantua "Hot Stove" League—eight teams in all. He continued to play with them in all age groups up through age 14. From 12-14 he hit an astounding .475, showing early signs of athletic talent.

"Jack used his own 31-in. Mickey Mantle bat," said ex-teammate Timothy Thomas. "Jack would kid the other players about using his bat. Some of them liked it real well. 'You'll have to wait till I'm finished with it,' Lambert would laugh. At least I think he was laughing."

Lambert was an Explorer Boy Scout from 1968-70. The troop met at the old church in Hiram [Ohio], and his mama was a troop den mother. One of his schoolmates, Roy Heaton, recalls being an Explorer Scout with him and, later, playing first-string guard with him in high school.

After turning left off Route 44 and onto Dudley Road, the Stanley residence came into view off in the distance. A ranch style structure standing about a quarter of a mile down the road, it's the second house on the left after passing a wide open segment of farm country. The long driveway to the back entrance seems like the length of a football field — a little hazardous in snowstorm road conditions on a cold, windy day.

Don Stanley was standing in the home's two-car garage leading to the back door. He seemed calm but enthusiastic as I got out of my blue Chevy S-10 pickup. At 2:00 p.m. everything was on schedule. We entered the house and I followed his example, taking off my wet shoes on the small concrete platform just inside the door. We walked stocking-footed up one step and turned left into the spacious kitchen where he offered me a seat at the kitchen table, a cookie and some coffee.

At age 66, Stanley was a retired grounds keeper from the Crestwood Local School District. Before that he was a farm manager 31 years. A former football/basketball player and track team member at Freedom High School, Don had been involved with sports most of his life. Medium-tall and slender, he still had a full head of gray hair, which was thinning a little. He looked a good 12 years younger than his age, had a smile across his face and in his eyes, too.

I was really fortunate to have visited so long with Don Stanley, fortunate too that he was so willing to reminisce about one of his favorite players. He was looking forward to having a copy of this book, but he died January 23, 1993, before it went to the printer.

When he spoke of Jack Lambert, Don Stanley's eyes took on that 1000-yard gaze of a man looking back on treasured memories. He <u>beamed</u> with pride whenever any mention was made of Jack's records. He talked about Lambert's first year in baseball:

"At first, he was afraid of being hit with the ball while at bat. Jack wouldn't stand solid in the batter's box. The coaches and I worked with him all year to break that habit. And the next year he became a very good hitter, hitting well over .400 each year in the league."

Under Head Coach Stanley, Jack played first base — batted left-handed and threw with his right. On occasion, he worked as the team's pitcher, for he had a strong arm. At bat, he knocked out a lot of line-drive singles and doubles and hot-footed it around the bases. Jack was serious about the game, someone had told me, but Stanley insisted he always took time to joke with teammates. According to Stanley, he was a kid easy to get along with, and the other kids liked him.

"Jack was one of the easiest kids to coach. All us coaches and players got along with him real well. He had a good attitude. A team player with a fine personality — a natural athlete."

One year, the team won both the little league championship and sportsmanship awards. To this day Lambert gives Coach Stanley credit for teaching him sportsmanship. Stanley also insisted on <u>teamwork</u> both in practice and during a game. That's something else Lambert promoted publicly during all his sports career.

After baseball, young Lambert played flag intramural football at Crestwood Middle School. The middle school didn't have any contact football, but flag-ball was a good fill-in until he began regular football as an 8th-grader.

Uncle Dan Harper recalled one of his nephew's first high

school games: "Jack got knocked out with a concussion. I don't remember which game it was, but he was only a freshman. He went right back in to play the next week. I wouldn't have done it, but that was Jack."

I wanted to know about his current life. I'd heard Jack had become a game warden. How did he get interested in the outdoors? In addition to football and baseball, Jack's interests turned to fishing and hunting—more hunting than fishing—from living on his grandpa's farm. Uncle Dan showed Jack how to hunt and fish when he was only ten—how to shoot a rifle and a shotgun—and also all he knew about gun safety. Jack practiced and became a good shot. He liked his grandfather's single-shot .22 best of all, but it turned up missing one day, and Jack never could find it. That always made him feel bad according to Uncle Dan. He shot a 12-gauge pump shotgun, too. He and Uncle Dan had fun picking off pigeons roosting right off the rafters inside the barn.

Out in the fields, they plugged plenty of rabbits and wood-chucks, sometimes a pheasant or two. The farm provided plenty of foliage for wildlife, with plenty of corn and row crops for game to munch on from nearby farms. Uncle Dan taught Jack how to clean his guns—and made <u>sure</u> they were clean, especially after a long day of hunting or shooting.

Reflecting on those days, Uncle Dan mused, "I think of Jack as a good friend. It was something we developed from living and hunting together. The hunting was fun and we'd be joking around on occasion. Especially when one or the other of us missed a shot. Couldn't let that go unnoticed."

Also, "I'll always remember how Jack's feet grew faster than the rest of him. And how his mother preached at him about not being a good loser." Laughing a little at the memories, "Jack despised losing at anything — baseball, football, ping-pong, anything. She'd say, 'You're not a good loser.' Then Jack would say, 'You show me a good loser, and I'll show you a <u>loser</u>.'"

Too bad Jack and his mama didn't have Lou Holtz's explanation of the difference between a "good loser" and a "good sport." When he was coaching at Arkansas, Holtz said it this way:

There is a big difference in being a good sport and a good loser. I don't want any athlete to ever play for us and be a good loser. A good loser says, "Well, we lost but we had a good time." I want the <u>good sport</u> to say, "I did the very best I could. We didn't win the football game. I give them credit for their success, but I am going to work harder until I become the best."

All that was part of growing up, and Jack's mother Joyce got her boy started in the right direction even though their ideas didn't agree all the time. Lambert's next challenge would come as Crestwood's starting quarterback. Maybe partly because of the hunting, he became a good shot at handing off the ball — and passing.

Chapter 11.

A Good Hander-Offer

Who Taught Him How?

It's true: Jack Lambert played quarterback in high school. The 6'5" skinny signal caller was also a defensive back. Playing both ways (offense and defense) — all the way—Lambert was an intense football player. As a quarterback, he led Crestwood High to an 8-1-1 record in 1969, his senior year. Who'd ever believe Lambert ever played quarterback? He did, although even in high school he claimed a first love for defense.

Head Coach Gerry Myers taught the Red Devils involved techniques. Rated a top Ohio high school football coach, Myers was a strict disciplinarian and an articulate instructor of football techniques, preaching goals to the team. Everybody said Lambert learned a lot from Coach Myers' teaching, gaining insight that lasted for years.

Myers was Crestwood's head football coach three years (1967-69). From there, he coached at the University of Dayton and Wayne High School in Dayton, Ohio, before retiring from the game. A 1963 graduate of Miami of Ohio, he played college football with another Northeast Ohio pro football player: Bill Triplett —who played with the St. Louis Cardinals, New York Giants, and Detroit Lions.

On a 30° February Sunday night Myers and I got together. It had been 46° earlier that day, warm for that time of year. The air was cool, damp, and had that penetrating effect that works on bones like WD-40 on an old rusty screw-bolt. Coach

Myers sat comfortably in his front room rocking chair while he talked about Jack Lambert. Softspoken and, occasionally, we could hear the quiet movement of the chair rocking back and forth. He chuckled and laughed in between his comments and sounded real proud of Lambert.

When not sitting, Myers stands 6'1-1/2", weighs 220, and has a full head of hair with a grey tinge. His laughter goes well with his round face, casual smile, and wire-rimmed glasses.

"The first time I saw Lambert was in the high school locker room," he recalled. "As I walked in to jot down names, he was sitting down. He introduced himself as Jack Lambert and said he wanted to play quarterback. I'd just got the coaching job and wanted to get organized as quick as possible. Practice would start the next day.

"He was a 5'9", 140-lb. sophomore at that time, but his feet were size 12. I couldn't believe the size of his feet! They seemed out of proportion with the rest of his body. We gave him jersey #11 to wear, and it was too big for his skinny frame. But that's all we had for him, and you couldn't see the number on his back with the jersey sagging on him. It looked about three sizes too big, and the numerals on the back went down each side of him. His teammates quickly nicknamed him <u>Sidestripes</u>.

"In his junior year, Lambert wanted to wear #00. I told him he had to be tough to wear that number. I told him 'You'll be a target, and everybody will be gunning for you.' That number stands out on the field. Well, he insisted he was tough, so I gave him #00. He wore it as a senior, too.

"He was a good student, with A's and B's. He could have been a straight-A student, but he wasn't dedicated to grades. He was popular, and you always see him at class reunions. Those are something I enjoy going to because of the memories of all the good times we had together.

"In football, Jack got by on determination. He wasn't an exceptional athlete and as a matter of fact, he wasn't our best athlete. But as a defensive back, he never got beat deep. On the field he was intense, all business, serious, had an instinct for the ball, and was a student of the game, but then Jack was a student of any sport: baseball, basketball, all of 'em.

"Jack was a leader, too, had no problems with leadership. As a matter of fact, all the kids were good students. We had no discipline problems.

"Thinking back, I'd say he was a tremendous leader and the kids would follow him. Jack was real confident and self-motivating. That's what made him great. There were other kids on the team with intensity, too. John Pennell was one of them. They were a great bunch of kids to coach, one of the few teams I've ever coached that had such intensity.

"Jack wasn't the greatest quarterback, but we lost only one game in his thirteen starts as the signal caller. He was quiet in the locker room before <u>and after</u> a game. He wasn't the rah-rah type of player. He just wasn't <u>exuberant</u> after we won.

"Jack's intensity and desire to play overcame his size and speed problems and, in all my years of coaching, he was the most intense player I ever coached. He is <u>very intelligent</u>, and he's proved that by being successful after he left pro football."

Intense? He really hammered on that <u>intense.</u> Since Myers was so influential in Lambert's career as a backfield player, I wanted to know more about him as a coach. What kind of man was this who influenced Jack Lambert in his teens? Jack's best buddy, John Pennell, filled me in:

"Coach Gerry Myers was a calm coach. He didn't rant or rave. He wasn't rah-rah, but he was strictly business. He shared a 10' x 10' office with his assistant coaches, and they covered the walls with sayings like 'You have to look good to play good.' He put posters in the locker room for the players to see.

"In his first year as coach, the players got new uniforms and equipment. It was supposed to make us players feel good about ourselves, build our morale so we'd play good in the game.

"Myers used trick plays to win important games. One play was the Double Zero (00), named after Lambert's jersey number. It worked like this: as we ran on and off the field to change personnel, we had only 10 players in the huddle. But as a part of double-zero, Mark Jakacki as he ran off the field didn't actually go off the field. He stood one foot inside the out-of-bounds stripe. Myers would tell the referees before a game about it, so they knew what was going on.

"Lambert would take the ball from center. Send Jakacki downfield, and try to hit him with a pass completion to set up Crestwood with good field position or the winning touchdown. Lambert didn't use the play in "The Impossible Dream Game" against state ranked (#7) Mogadore. Crestwood was severely underdogged but we came out shooting! After the second half kickoff, Crestwood had the ball.

"As a good leader, Lambert marched the Red Devils, from their own 44-yard line, down field on running and passing plays in to scoring position. We scored the winning touchdown on a belly play around end and upset Mogadore 16-8. The next day sports headlines red: 'The Impossible Dream Comes True!' The win made the 1968 season real nice!

"Of course, Myers' halftime speeches helped fire-up our team for victory. On one occasion, Coach Myers looked mad—one of the very few times he ever looked that way—and he threatened the team, 'Don't you lose this game. If you do, don't you show up for the homecoming dance...or maybe even history class!'

"Teaching history was easier for Myers than coaching football, and the athletes got by in his class. It was a laid back, relaxed atmosphere. Everybody who took the class got by. Myers' instruction consisted of lecturing and reading, without intense pressure. He was an easy grader and, if you showed up, you probably would at least pass.

"When it came to coaching, things went a little different. Myers commanded respect from the players. We were impressionable, and he made a real _impression_ as a 6' 1-1/2" former college tight end. He was a big man with a crew cut, and we players knew who the boss was. He had 'presence.'

"One example will tell you about Myers's _presence_. In his first year at Crestwood, the sophomore team was a close-knit group with a lot of talent, as they proved in their three years playing together. Everybody called them the 'Super Sophs' because of their size and ability. Well, before summer practice, Myers walked into the dressing room sporting a new crew cut.

In a calm voice he said, 'Everyone will get a butch hair cut.' Even though his voice didn't match his commanding appearance, the boys knew to take him seriously.

"Thing was: everything was <u>his</u> way or no way, so everybody and anybody associated with the team got a crew cut. The next year, the crew cut was optional, and the fellows went back to their regular haircuts. It was the same with the unbalanced line: it went by the wayside also from the year before. With a change in talent, Crestwood shifted to a balanced line formation in Lambert's junior and senior years. It was all something like musical chairs.

"And <u>music</u>: all during the Crestwood days, Myers <u>always</u> played music in the dressing room before practice and before a game. In the coaches' office, he had records and a player connected to speakers in the locker room. We got dressed to the tune of one of the coach's favorites, 'The Cotton Boll Song.' That's not the official title of the song—maybe Cotton <u>Bowl</u>?—It probably had something to do with growing cotton.

"Before a game, Coach Myers told the team the first three or four plays they would run. He usually called the offensive plays, but on occasion, Jack called a play. I sometimes helped him decide—like '32 Wham over Pennell,' when I (at right tackle) knew I could take my man out. Or '32 Belly Pass' with the halfback following the fullback through the hole, then stretching into the right flat for a pass from the quarterback.

"How did Myers dress? A baseball cap, a Red Devil football sweater, coach's pants and black shoes. He always wore sweaters. He came from home in 'em, he taught history in 'em, he coached in 'em. He went home in 'em and went out in the evenings in 'em. He wore headphones to talk with coaches in the press box in the stands.

"He didn't pace the sidelines and he wasn't nervous. He didn't jump around like some coaches do. He motivated from the practice field and locker room. At halftime, he drew plays on the board, stuff that needed to be discussed or adjusted, going over the game plan and talking defense.

"But if you were just plain screwing up out there, you could expect punishment in practice. Like, you could expect to run six to ten 100-yard gassers — what a hot, tiring, everlasting drill! It motivated you, and Coach Myers would be there hollering, 'You're doggin' it! Pick it up and let's go!' But he wasn't obnoxious or abusive about it.

"Another thing was the 'belly button pad.' It was just a small round pad, but it embarrassed a player into changing his behavior, because he'd have to wear this goofy-looking pad over his belly button <u>in practice</u> for mistakes in a game. One lineman always used to stand up when he blocked. It was a habit he'd picked up, but it's a big no-no in football. So this guy had plenty of chances to wear the belly-button pad. Naturally, Coach knew when to get on his players and when not to. Loafers pissed him off more than anything else. He sometimes put loafers through little team-oriented punishments: if one player dogged it, Coach punished the whole unit or team. Loafers got the message <u>real quick</u>.

"Of course it was o.k. to be <u>cocky</u>. Myers <u>encouraged</u> us to be cocky, especially on the field because it intimidated the opposing team and gained a psychological edge. And sharpness: that was another of Myers's pet peeves: if his players didn't <u>look</u> sharp. He believed in 'Look Sharp. Play Sharp.' If anybody looked sloppy, it would be, 'Give me 10 quick push-ups! Give me 10 quick sit-ups!' "

The bottom line is: Myers has the best honor any coach can receive — he is remembered and highly respected by his former players.

So that's where he got it: the cocky attitude, the sharp dresser, never loafing, always driving hard. Don't ever wonder where a ball player got his moves or perfected his attitudes: somewhere back there he had a coach...

Another of Lambert's former-Crestwood teammates, Tom Cofojohn, recalls, "Coach Myers was strong on discipline, he taught Jack and all of us good. He was the one who taught Jack how far he could go in football." Cofojohn was sitting in the kitchen of his country home, drinking coffee while discussing Lambert over the phone.

He remembered that once, after a poor showing in a scrimmage against Youngstown McDonald, Coach Myers punished the squad with ten 100-yard gassers, a grueling drill on a humid, sultry day. But Lambert was enthusiastic, out in front, leading the pack — hollering and pushing fellow squad members to give it their all. Already a leader. Why? Can't you hear it? *We shouldn'ta lost that game and they were part of why. Hey, this is <u>serious</u>. Coach says it's part of my responsibility to make us a winning team...Pick it up — pick it up! Let's go.. let's go!* So Myers was the role model, the one everybody said was a major influence.

As a quarterback, Lambert thought of himself as a good "hander-offer," not a good passer. That's debatable. Cofojohn described Lambert as a stand-up quarterback "who did a fine job handing-off the ball. When passing, he just took the ball from center, stepped back three steps, and fired it to a receiver." He often completed those throws.

Uncle Dan Harper had called him "a good short passer. He was good on those 30-40 yard passes," although he believed his nephew had a much stronger arm and could've thrown long. Lambert himself once said, "I was a good hander-offer as a quarterback. But I liked defense much more. I loved hitting other people rather than being hit."

With his reputation of <u>not</u> being an outstanding quarterback, the 6'5" 175-lb. Lambert said, "...my best time for the 40-yard dash back then was six seconds flat. S-l-o-w. When we flip-flopped, though, I played defensive halfback, and even then I loved to hit. Loved it."

A hitter for sure. The lanky defender showed it in a game against Rootstown High. When the opposing quarterback, Eskridge, rolled out on a bootleg, Lambert came full throttle from the secondary. He made a crushing clothesline tackle near the sideline. The runner gained nothing and was "out of commission." Eskridge felt like he'd met a Mack truck head-on, and apparently Lambert was upset about hurting his opponent, really felt <u>bad</u> about it.

Cofojohn told me, "Jack was <u>real upset</u> and felt hurt about knocking the guy out."

Lambert continued to play aggressively and well the rest of the season. All through high school, people used the term "intense" to describe him. Anyway you slice it, "intense" means extreme — one way to become an outstanding football player. Jack's attitude or manner on the field was new to Crestwood football fans. But to him, it was normal, a characteristic he'd had since childhood, from days as a little guy playing backyard sports and later playing Little League ball.

Will anybody ever know exactly why Jack Lambert was so intense? Did Lambert himself know the answer? It would take years of peeling back the onion-skin layers of his memory to know exactly why. Yet we can honestly say, that intensity was always part of his personality. Even Uncle Dan Harper spoke of Jack's excessive energy. He remembered Jack's determination from when he was a little fellow. Uncle Larry Marek agreed. "Lambert was intense as far back as I can remember." Remember that term — "need to achieve?"

In high school, the skinny signal caller wanted (or needed) to be the best. Maybe he didn't achieve that need as an offensive player, but he sure did on defense. It seemed to be his attitude toward football. He put maximum effort into practice or a game, more than any of his teammates. He knew an "excessive" approach would make him outstanding — plus he had a weight disadvantage to overcome. He had to play hard.

You could see it when he made a tackle. A smashing hard hitter—he knocked a couple of players out, drove a few back for minus yardage, and caused ball carriers to fumble. Other players didn't hit with such intensity. They tackled hard enough to take an opponent down, but not enough to knock him out, or cause fumbles and lost yardage.

Sports psychology gets down to the fact that intense player-behavior varies in degrees, depending on the individual. Other hard-hitting linebackers do exist. Do they all play at the same level of intensity? No! Take Bob Babich, for example, former middle-linebacker for San Diego and, later, Cleveland. He played intense football for Campbell Memorial High School, another school in Northeast Ohio. Babich's intensity was more pronounced than that of his teammates. Like Lambert, Babich wanted to be "the best," and it showed in his middle-school to high school-level sports.

When tackling, Babich never appeared determined to knock a player out. Fans recognized his aggressive style, and on occasion he threw a runner for a loss—or caused a fumble. He was just known as intense "in a different way."

Lambert also played "aggressive." Is it innate in a personality or is it learned? The experts have different points of view. Some say it's born in a guy. Some say it's learned. Some hedge by saying it's both. To some specialists, aggressive behavior is always violent. Others see it as excessiveness in any social situation. Still others believe it's an element of any contact sport — almost a requirement for sports like football and hockey.

Research demonstrates that physical punishment is associated with high aggression in children. It is reported that strong physical punishment in the home is a characteristic part of the background of [aggression]...

But in football, aggressive behavior is taught. Coaches teach their players to assert themselves aggressively—from the midget leagues to upper-level athletics. We know that at least somewhere down the line some aggressive play is learned. Everybody agrees that Lambert's coaches at Crestwood High taught aggressive football. Jack understood their reasoning: in order to win, achieve goals, and meet challenges, you gotta be aggressive. Every high school player has heard it: "Our team has to attack those guys (the opposition) with 110% effort!"

High school players learn in a hurry that their opponents will be aggressive. "If you're timid, he'll knock your block off!" Force against force, the strongest wins. A law of physics? In football psychology, they call it "controlled aggression" because of the rules that govern the game — with rule infractions and regulated play enforced by qualified officials. Players learn about controlled aggression, too, from a coach's speeches about penalty violations that hurt the whole team. A player "out of control" can cause a team defeat.

Lambert played aggressive football, both by instinct and by coaches' training, but usually "under control." He stretched his luck as far as it could without getting penalized.

Sometimes, he pushed beyond the game's limitations, and the ref threw a flag on him: 15 yards!

He sparked Crestwood to an upset triumph over state-ranked Mogadore. The same old intense Lambert helped win in a Garrettsville game—one of those traditional rivalries. Although both teams had friends on both sides, everybody came out hitting—all for inter-community bragging rights. Jack hit hard. Like they say, he had "no friends on the field"—causing runners to fumble. Often. That was his style. In the locker room before a game he prepared himself emotionally. He keyed himself up, slapping heads with other players.

According to Tom Cofojohn, "Jack was a team leader, very intense and emotional before game time. Although maybe an hour earlier he'd be horsing around, joking was always at the right place and time. Never right before the game."

John Madden spoke to this point in Hey, Wait A Minute.

He'd been trying to get all his players to be serious before a game. As he tells it:

"But Blair Sheldon stopped in my office. 'Coach,' he said, 'there are all different kinds of personalities in that locker room before a game. Everybody wants to win the same way but there are different ways of preparing to win. Some guys take a nap, some go to the bathroom, some throw up, some listen to music. Some, like me, tell jokes. We're not all the same'...After that, I always had two locker rooms...one for the quiet guys, one for the guys who liked to play music or tell jokes."

ANY OTHER INSIGHTS

On a bright, hot day in August, just a few days before school started the weather was humid as Northeast Ohio usually is. I parked at Jackson High School in Jackson Township, just five miles north of Massillon — big football country. Entering the main doors and through the front corridor, a huge skin of a polar bear loomed ahead in a case. Ah, yes! The school symbol…animal…the "Fighting Polar Bears." I was early and everything was relatively quiet. An adjacent hallway led to the principal's office.

Rick Campbell was the assistant principal in charge of student attendance. Tall with a stocky build, Campbell looked to be in his mid 40's. His short-sleeve shirt and light-weight slacks seemed appropriate for a school official during summer hours.

Like most school administrators, his desk was scattered with official school papers and books. Leaning back in his executive-model chair, he began to talk about his old teammate, Jack Lambert. He was proud of having known Lambert and obviously enjoyed talking about those days when they played together.

"Lambert made a personal commitment to winning. He was goal-oriented and was out to be Number One. He was always out to improve his talent. He played hard-nose football, was intense, never backed down from a challenge." Campbell speaks with authority and is convincing. Recent contact with his old teammate? No. These were memories from long ago. But they are memories tempered with adult evaluations — from both an educator's and a coach's point of view.

1969: On to a new challenge with the Chagrin Falls game, a tough opponent. They'd defeated Crestwood in the season's finale 26-14, but not without a fight. Lambert established a running game by handing the ball off to his backfield. But in the third period, his team was down 14-6. When Lambert started the drive, being an ordinary hander-offer wasn't good enough. Jack finished the drive with a 17-yard touchdown pass to tight end Rick Campbell and the team added 2 extra points that ended Crestwood's scoring. More than that, Lambert finished the game with 10 completions for 137 yards. As Campbell told it, "not bad for someone who considered himself just a hander-offer."

In his final high school year, Lambert turned into a fiery winner, leading his team to a PCL co-championship. Today Kenneth Evans is a guidance counselor at Crestwood. He remembers Lambert as a high school economics student and ball player since he was Lambert's assistant football coach:

"Jack was a good athlete. All-Portage County first team in football, basketball, and baseball (as a catcher). He was quarterback and played defensive back; he made first team All PCL as a defensive back. Jack had good football <u>sense</u>. He had a good sense of anticipation of where the play was going and he was <u>very</u> aggressive as a tackler.

"He was an average student, but in economics he did better than average in my class. Jack had a good understanding about money."

Money was something he probably learned about from being around his folks's florist shop, located in Mantua.

Reflecting on the past that afternoon at Jackson High, Rick Campbell mused, "What Lambert did in football was just phenomenal. He wasn't a fast runner in the 40. To rise to his heights...well, it's just phenomenal. But Jack always had <u>focus</u>. A focus on sports <u>goals</u> and how to reach them. He knew what he wanted and went all-out for it. As a classmate, so far as I could see, Jack was a <u>private</u> person. He knew how to be friendly, but he kept his distance, too."

Off the field, most folks said Lambert was just a normal teenager, willing to take a dare. In school his friends were other athletes, all of them sometimes going to Kent or Ravenna for fun. Mantua didn't have much for kids to do outside of sports. <u>Work</u> was always available on one of the local farms.

Just a normal teenager? Coach Myers had mentioned John Pennell as another <u>intense</u> ball player along with Lambert, so I got in touch with him again to talk about normal teenagers.

During their elementary and junior-high school years: John said Jack used to go roller-skating at St. Joseph's Church in Mantua. John remembered when Jack won the pass, punt, and kick contest in Mantua. Even at that early age, Jack's dream was to play pro football.

They were high school seniors the same year. Pennell was first team All-Portage County tackle for Crestwood in 1969 and he was also on the wrestling team when John was Jack's closest friend.

"Jack and I would hustle the girls, too. Jack's steady girl

friend in high school was a cheerleader, and he spent a lot of time with her.

"Jack and I played baseball together in high school. After the games, we drove around in Lambert's old blue Nova. Can't remember if it was a '65 or '66.

"Earlier? Well, back in 1972-73, we got into a fight at the Crazy Horse Saloon. This guy hit Jack on the head with a beer bottle. I heard the bottle break. I turned and punched the guy 15 or 20 times — and he ran out the door! He took off running, didn't want any more. Jack had a cut across his head with some bleeding, but he was o.k."

"A normal teenager?" This isn't a story of a saint. What about other sports? Being tall, Lambert was a good basketball player — played forward, averaging 17 points per game under Head Coach Bill Cox. Coach Cox remarked, in an interview, "Jack played basketball with <u>zero emotion</u>, just the opposite of how he played football. But he had a lot of skill and played with his head. Smart."

Lanky Lambert was helpful in Crestwood's upset victory over Hudson Local that year. Hudson players took the Red Devils lightly, drinking soda pop and laughing as Crestwood walked into the lockers. A happy time — but they weren't laughing when the game was over. Cox said Lambert was real serious all the time:

"He was businesslike—'Yes sir, Coach', or, 'No sir, Coach'. Always respected the coaches and teachers. And always had school books with him to study. He was a model player in all three sports.

"Jack was in awe of famous athletes and wanted to be one. He played the best he could — gave 110% effort in practice or a game. Sometimes he played harder in practice than he played in a game. A coach didn't have to say his name twice for him to hit the field. Once he heard the first vowel sound of his name, Lambert was gone. On the field!"

In baseball, he was a good catcher who liked to get into the dirt and dig out bad pitches. Block the plate for oncoming runners where the action was.

Ken Evans, the assistant football coach, recalled that Coach Myers arranged a field trip to the Pro Football Hall of Fame. The whole football team went just before Lambert's senior year. Evans said it was an inspiration for all of them, and what a future would follow that trip! As it turned out, football recognition did follow the hander-offer. Making All-PCL in three sports, Lambert also claimed other accolades. He won three letters in football, two in basketball, and four in baseball. He captained the football, basketball, and baseball teams in his senior year.

Wisconsin was the only Big Ten school that showed any interest in him for college play. Miami of Ohio under Head Coach Bill Mallory didn't offer Lambert a full scholarship. The same was true for Ohio University.

Years later Mallory commented on his decision: "I've taken a lot of kidding about that, but nobody really knew anything about Jack at the time." Later when Lambert was a perennial All-Pro linebacker for Pittsburgh, Mallory remembered that he was coaching at Miami when Lambert was graduated from Crestwood:

"A friend brought me a film of a game that showed this skinny kid running around the field making tackles. But it was so bad and scratchy, you really couldn't tell that much. It was like one of those old-time movies with Charlie Chaplin making jerky little movements. I offered Lambert a third of a scholarship, but then Kent State gave him a full ride."

Those were the extent of Lambert's scholarship offers. Jack accepted the Kent State deal, going on to make football history in the Mid-American Conference.

CHAPTER III
THE STORK

YOU GOTTA BE A FOOTBALL HERO...

As #99 at Kent State he picked up a reputation for being mean and aggressive. He also picked up a nickname.

Kids pick up nicknames. Heard a while back about a tall Scandihoovian kid in his hometown. Everybody called him the "Blond Blizzard." The fellow telling the story was near-sighted, wore thick glasses, and walked with a limp: so they called him the "Blind Buzzard." He still answers to "Hey, Buzz!"

Kent State teammates nicknamed Jack "The Stork," referring to All-Pro linebacker Ted Hendricks. So many similarities. Hendricks participated in eight Pro-Bowl games, seven conference championship games, and four Super Bowls. Indestructible at 6'7", only 235 pounds and, apparently, he and Lambert played with the same temperament, the same inner drive. John Madden once described Hendricks:

"When he blitzed from the weak side, a running back couldn't block him. And even against a tight end, he was a great blitzer...Ted dominated a tight end. If he wanted to get by the tight end, he got by him. If he didn't want the tight end to get off the line of scrimmage, the tight end didn't get off."

Sounds like a description of Lambert when he was with the Steelers, doesn't it? Jack weighed much less than Hendricks, but still became an indomitable force in college. In 1970, Head Coach Dave Puddington recruited Jack to Kent State. "We got Lambert for half a scholarship," Puddington said. "Ohio University offered him books, so we upped the ante to half a scholarship." So little, yet so much!. Both Miami and Ohio Universities lost the bidding war for a student-athlete, one who would later play in the NFL.

We can get a feel for yesteryear's small state college football programs by remembering another Kent State football player who enrolled there 15 years earlier than Lambert: terrifying fellow named Louis Leo "Lou" Holtz. At 5'10", weighing 135 lbs., Lou Holtz wore No. 52 on his blue and gold uniform and played center-linebacker from 1955-57. *Linebacker?* Knee surgery after his junior year had knocked him out of football; he couldn't play during his senior year (1958). His path into big-time football back then was about as far from Jack Lambert's as you could get. Growing up in East Liverpool, Ohio, graduating No. 234 in his high school class of 278, he'd thought the good life would be a used Chevy and a job in the steel mill, but his parents pestered him into going to college. In a 1982 interview, Holtz laughed, "You hear people talk about having an inferiority complex...Me? I didn't have a complex. Plainly, I was inferior."

Holtz remembered that the KSU varsity used to play against its alumni for one of its spring games. "In one spring alumni game, I played opposite my old fraternity brother, Bill Mclain. No one knew it, but Bill told me where the plays were going," and Holtz the "intense linebacker" had the greatest game of his entire college career. He earned a varsity "K" in football that fall.

But back to 1970: Lambert reported to Kent's training camp as a defensive end. He played that position during his freshman and sophomore years. Although freshmen weren't eligible to play for Kent at the time, his coaches said the Stork put out 110% effort in training. In training camp the following year, Lambert again played aggressively, and his style caught the eye of new Head Coach Don James. James's assistants also were impressed, especially Dennis Fitzgerald, the team's defensive coach. James promptly put Lambert on a full scholarship at defensive end. They still thought he was a light-weight at that position.

"I don't think he ever was over 200 with us," James declared. "When we first weighed in, when Jack was a sopho-more, he was 188. Jack just made up for it."

He overcame his weight disadvantage with an older, tougher version of the same "controlled aggression" he'd learned in high school.

"He's such an intense individual that, if he was playing domi-noes, he would beat the spots off them to get the right number," added Fitzgerald. A few years after Lambert was out of college, Fitzgerald was remembering: "He had the best lateral quick-ness and peripheral vision of anyone on the squad. When tack-ling an opponent, he had the ability to gather himself and un-coil like a snake."

While playing defensive end those two years, Lambert per-formed well and racked up some impressive numbers: in beat-ing on-coming blockers he made 59 solo tackles and 88 assisted. A total of 147. That's a lot of tackles. After the season, he re-ceived Kent's "Outstanding Sophomore" award from the Alumni Association. To stay in shape, he played softball that summer.

At the beginning of the '72 campaign, a young player named Bobby Bender was Kent's ace middle-linebacker. On a moment's notice, three weeks before opening day, Bender quit football. He decided it wasn't his game. Packed it in and left town. Some of us look back at the chronology of events and we never can pinpoint the specific moment or the particular event that changed the course of our lives. What if this...or what if that? Jack Lambert will never have to wonder about all those what if's. If Bender hadn't left town three weeks before opening day of that football season, Lambert might never have played middle-linebacker. What a difference that would have made, not only in Lambert's life but also in Steeler and American foot-ball history.

Don James soon evaluated Jack's potential for the position. Making the shift from defensive end to middle-linebacker was crucial for Lambert. Weight-wise, he was at a disadvantage. At best, he probably tipped the scales at 190 soaking-wet. But his aggressive performance and intense demeanor helped him make the change. Picture a cougar crouched down low, staring, concentrating. Steady, eyes focused—then <u>pouncing</u>.

Without much time to prepare, The Stork took on the challenge of filling the middle-linebacker slot. It took sweat and grime, but Jack knew all about hard work from summers on his grandfather's farm. The gangling linebacker trained like a Marine recruit, getting ready for combat. Under the tutelage of Coach Fitzgerald, he was ready to be Kent's new linebacker for the opening game of the 1972 season. At the same time, Fitzgerald became The Stork's favorite coach. Forever. Even to this day.

According to Jack's mother, Joyce, "His favorite coach was always Dennis Fitzgerald, because they were very much alike. And because he taught Jack so much about playing the game."

The Stork became the Golden Flashes' best-ever middle-backer, one of the best in the Mid-American Conference, and arguably the best ever to play in the NFL. Nobody denies that it was an incredible achievement for him to be ready in such a short period. More than that the Stork was intrigued by the opportunity, the possibilities this position held for a career. As the season unfolded, Jack went "on to the halls of glory." Like "to the shores of Tripoli."

One of Lambert's best games was in Kent's 37-14 trouncing of Ohio University. Playing like a man possessed, the Stork blasted through the middle to block a punt. "Every time they gain an inch, he feels responsible," quipped James. Lambert finished the game with 10 solo tackles and five assists, a pass interception, and a blocked punt for a safety. The week before, in Kent's 14-10 win over Bowling Green, Lambert had gathered 10 solo tackles and 11 assists!

Lambert and I were in school at Kent State at the same time and I saw that Bowling Green game. I remember seeing #99 on that blue and gold uniform making tackles all over the field and dropping back on pass coverage.

"[He was] a somewhat puny 6'5" 189-pounder out of high school as a quarterback...I knew from the time I first saw him and he began working in the agility program that he was going to be a great football player," said Coach Fitzgerald.

What About Off the Field?

Jack's prospects on the field were great. But what about Lambert off the field? A friendly guy, believe it or not. Big tall blond with a blond mustache — he sometimes "talked with his hands" and was cordial, not mean like people in the media later made him out to be. Jack used to stop by the K.S.U. Student Health Center (hospital) to visit an injured teammate or just to joke around like one fall day when The Stork walked into the Health Center and spotted floor nurse Pat Hively.

Hively had bright red hair, inherited from her Scottish ancestors—not from a bottle of Loving Care. You couldn't miss her and she had difficulty hiding out. Pat glowed like a summer sunrise, and everyone called her "Red." She remembered one day she heard Lambert bellow:

"Are you pill-pushers still here?"

"Why of course. How are you today, Jack?"

"Fine, just fine. Just stopped to say hello." But it wasn't just to say "hello." Never was. What he liked was to tease Hively about her boys, Buddy and Mike, who played football for Field High School, a competitor of Crestwood's in Portage County.

"What's the name of that place where your boys play? Oh, yeah! That's out there where all the farmers live." Much laughter.

"So where do you get off? Where do you think you live? Mantua's nothin' but hayseed country. You've got a heck of a lot more farmers than we do!" She didn't give an inch. Everyone standing around began to laugh. Kidding, easy-going, Jack was easy to get along with.

What about Lambert off the field? Ask ten different people and you'll get ten different answers. Some folks won't talk, some will. A split-decision.

Between quarters at K.S.U., Jack sometimes worked as a utility fill-in for Samuel Moore and Company. "Jack would stack material, box stuff, and work as a helper," according to Roger Ware, a fellow employee. "He was a hard worker, real serious about his job, and he listened to other employees and supervisors. His mother worked for the company, too," Ware added. "She was a super person with a great personality. Very outgoing but serious about her work. Jack and his mother were alike. When it was time to get something done, they didn't fool around. They got it done."

The season rolled down and it became a must for Kent to win their last two games if they were to win the M.A.C. championship and a trip to the Tangerine Bowl. Two tough opponents still stood in their way — Miami and Toledo. On to victory! Knowing they had to win, The Stork led the defense in the Flashes' 21-10 victory at Oxford.

Late in the game, Miami rolled into scoring position with Bob Hitches' running. On fourth down, the Redskins gave to Hitches once more, but the Stork read the play. *"Ha! Hitches, you'll get it again and I'll stop you in your tracks. You ain't gonna gain an inch, Hot Shot! I'll be stopping your number cold and the rest of our defense will be right there on the assists. Come 'n get it...come 'n get it...".*

He busted in on Miami, hit Hitches hard, and gave the rest of the defense time to assist and they stopped Hitches from scoring. At game's end, Lambert had compiled 19 solo tackles and five assists.

Next came Toledo. Same old Lambert. Self-propelled. The Golden Flashes knocked off Toledo 27-9, while Lambert tallied 15 solo hits. That fine performance won him the Defensive Player of the Game, the fifth such award during the season.

The Flashes took off next for Tampa and the Tangerine Bowl. There a mistake-riddled Kent, with seven turnovers, lost a heartbreaker to the University of Tampa, 21-18. Yet the amazing Stork led Kent's defense with his usual controlled aggressive style. For his outstanding performance, he earned the game's MVP Award on Defense. If his response ran true to form he must have been thinking, *"Yeah, o.k. so the Tangerine Bowl MVP is good, but it don't mean much without the win. We shoulda won it! How could we lose such an important game?..."*

Kent finished the year with a 6-5-1 overall, a 4-1 M.A.C. mark. Lambert made 117 solo tackles and 116 assists for a year's total of 233. Awards? Named first team All-M.A.C. on defense, M.A.C. Defensive Player of the Year, Kent's Most Valuable Defensive Player, and Kent's Best Linebacker. Jack also earned honorable mention on that year's All-American team.

What a year! But The Stork would have to wait for the next season to "be himself" and be <u>openly visible</u> on the gridiron.

AND BETWEEN SEASONS?

Always planning, looking ahead, how did Lambert spend the off season? When he wasn't working construction, you could have found him at Dix Stadium, pumping iron — something he did with relish to add strength—and weight. His lean, tall body, was still 30 to 40 lbs. lighter than most middle-linebackers.

The difficulty Jack had in adding weight tells us something about Jack himself and about the weight-training/strength-building programs in colleges and with pro-teams of the middle 1970's. Bill Walsh has touched on it in his book, <u>Building a Champion.</u>

Had coaches been aware of steroids' positive effects, they might have actually endorsed them. Extended planned programs of steroid use can result in as much as a 20 percent gain in strength and explosion, a marked increase in speed and quickness—and a significant negative personality change.

Typically a 240-pound man will reach a weight of 265 pounds.

But the side effects can be insidious. The athlete becomes much more aggressive and much more intense, almost out of control on the field... [with] <u>severe</u> problems off the field.

We all know from the sad conclusion to another pro player, Lyle Alzado, in 1992. Alzado wanted to be one of the best, too, and took "roids" to add body/muscle-weight. He didn't realize he was self-destructing all the time he was aiming to be the toughest, meanest, <u>best</u> guy in pro football.

Jack didn't <u>need</u> any more aggression or explosive quickness. He needed extra pounds. The fact that he didn't put on the weight easily indicated that neither he nor the Kent trainers and coaches were into steroids for <u>any</u> reason.

That summer of '73, in the evenings, you'd often find Jack at "The Crazy Horse," one of Kent's night spots. Most all the KSU jocks went there—to down a cold one, or play pinball—or some of the other games. All the regulars at The Crazy Horse knew each other at least enough to say "hi". That included me. I remember Lambert always said, "Hello, Big Guy!" I always answered, "Whatta ya say, Jackson?" Lambert loved those games! He played a lot of foozball and...just about any game in the house. He played against his teammates or against anybody willing to oblige. Whoever was foolish enough...since Lambert was out to win. He played those games like he did football. He didn't take losing kindly.

During a couple of summers, Lambert worked for a construction company building the Richfield Coliseum. He operated an air hammer (jack hammer), a piece of equipment to test any operator's endurance, drilling out concrete surfaces. Heavy air tools like jack hammers vibrate the body, throwing dust all around. Those summers, Lambert often looked like a mine worker. He didn't blister, but because he has such a light complexion, he burned from the scorching sun.

That last summer, after work, The Stork played softball again. They respected him as a good hitter and fielder. When the game was over, Lambert and his buddies usually went out on the town. Lambert had a smart-mouth, cocky attitude (still does). If he was upset, he wouldn't pound on a table: he would just "tell somebody off." He had kind of a soft laugh, but he kept that tough-guy image he'd picked up years before. He and the softball team would hit some of the local bars and let the good times roll.

I never saw him in a fight at The Crazy Horse, but I understand that, on occasion, the "Boys from Mantua" mixed it up in a barroom brawl. All it took was a smart remark from a stranger — or someone who couldn't hold his beer — at a nearby grog shop. The Stork and his friends couldn't let it go; just too macho. Sparks would fly. According to comrade Cofojohn, "We got into some fights in the bars. But nobody ever got hurt...maybe a bloody nose or two."

LAST YEAR AT KENT

1973, his senior year, Lambert topped 6'5" and 205. Up from 190. He helped Kent State to a 9-2 record, the best in the university's history. But a disappointing 20-10 loss to Miami (0.) cost Kent the M.A.C. championship. A shivering 27,363 fans crowded Dix Stadium on that cold, snowy day — the largest crowd ever to watch the Golden Flashes. During the third period, the towering Stork threw Miami's quarterback Sanna for a loss. Out came the referee's flag, Kent was penalized 15 yards. The Redskins took advantage of the infraction and collected the dividends of victory. Can't blame that on another soul.

Somebody asked Lambert about the violation. "On the play, I nailed their quarterback and then I saw the flag go down," he answered. "I asked the referee what I did and he said, 'You hit the quarterback too hard!' I asked him if it was an illegal hit and he said 'No.'"

In top form, The Stork gathered 20 solo tackles and nine assists. Lambert's high school buddy, Rick Campbell, was right: that kind of record is flat <u>phenomenal</u>. He even out-played his counterpart, "Apache" Jerald Tillman, who made 10 solo tackles and six assists.

Regardless of his outstanding performances, Lambert had some critics. Former Cleveland Browns linebacker Vince Costello, a coach for the Cincinnati Bengals spoke at the Hall of Fame luncheon in Canton before the Miami game. Someone asked him a question about Lambert's ability. Costello stated unequivocally that "Kent State's Jack Lambert has neither the size nor the ability to ever play in the NFL." Lambert had the last word on <u>that</u> score. Learning what Costello said, he must have thought, *"Why that sorry fool! Where does he get off? I'll prove he's wrong and blasted his negative opinion! He'll eat those words some day."* <u>Sic transit</u> Vince Costello.

His mind was set on Pro Football—at least as far as the Kent staff knew. Louise Harper laughs about it. "Jack always said if he didn't make it in football, he could always become a plumber." But secretly, she told me, he <u>really</u> wanted to play hockey. She claimed that he always wanted to play hockey more than he did football, and these days he plays amateur hockey in and around Pittsburgh.

"When he was young, his grandfather Lambert took him to watch hockey games," Louise Harper remembered. "Grandpa Lambert was a detective for the Higbee Company and he got free tickets to hockey games. He took Jack with him, and Jack's interest grew from there."

After the Bowling Green game, The Stork sat quietly in a chair just inside the Kent American Legion Hall. He appeared to be private, tranquil, and resting after that hard game. It must have taken a lot out of him, for he had seemed to just barely have enough energy left to speak to passers-by. Who knows what he was thinking? What's curious is that nobody stopped to ask. Bruised and tired, he was still so goal-oriented he was probably thinking about prospects in Pro Football...or re-playing the Bowling Green game in his head.

Coach James commented during the season: "Right now, Jack's as good a prospect [for a pro team] as there is. He's strong for being tall," said James. "He's very quick and has good range."

Football was where the action was at Kent State. Even in practice he seemed determined that everything should "go right." One day, the squad was going through Coach James's "nut-cracker drill" — a version of the three-on-three drill used by most college coaches. With a sudden burst of speed Lambert came storming out of the drill. Something was bothering him. In seconds The Stork descended on the center, Henry Waszczuk. Latching onto his face mask, Lambert thundered, "You held me on all three plays in that drill, and if you do it again, I'll kill you!" Henry never held him again.

"He had complete disdain for pain. He played in games that many would have missed. He played in one game with hip-pointers on both hips, a bruised chest, and a swollen elbow," recalled Coach Fitzgerald. "You could sense that winning was v-e-r-y important to him. And he was a very unselfish player."

It all paid off with the honors Jack received at the end of the year:

Named one of Kent's tri-captains,

Named to first team All M.A.C. (for second year),

Named to third team All-American,

Named Kent's Best Linebacker, and winner of Kent's MVP on Defense Award.

Played in All-Ohio Shrine Game, North-South Game, and All-American Bowl Game.

After that the Pittsburgh Steelers drafted The Stork in the second round of the 1974 NFL pro-draft. A few years later in a rare gesture of respect, Kent State retired Lambert's famous #99, one of only three football jersey numbers Kent has ever retired. The others belonged to Jim Corrigall, who played years of Pro Football in Canada and Eric Wilkerson.

The Varsity "K" also inducted Lambert [as it did Lou Holtz -(February 1990)] into its Sports Hall of Fame in February 1981. Later the Mid American Conference inducted him into its M.A.C. Hall of Fame. Today, Kent State gives its Lambert Cup Award in spring practice each year to the most outstanding defensive player.

PHOTO COURTESY KENT STATE UNIVERSITY

JACK LAMBERT #99

CHAPTER IV
THE LAST FIVE SECONDS

After his senior football season, Lambert began a strenuous weight training program, doing bench presses up to 375 lbs., repetitions of curls, and other exercises. Plus wind sprints and jogging to add strength, coordination, and flexibility. The pressure was on to gain weight, for The Stork was at a serious weight disadvantage at 200 lbs. His aim was to gain at least 25 lbs. in preparation for pro football. More pounds were absolutely necessary. Most pro teams in the 1974 draft emphasized the fact.

Lambert wasn't sure who would draft him, but he knew there was a good chance he would be selected by someone. Work continued at Kent's Dix Stadium, and the intense competitor pumped iron again and again. Over his head, hour after hour, day by day, and weeks at a time. He had to reach his weight goal and be ready for that first training camp. Jack's ultimate endeavor, was to play pro football. It was his childhood dream — had been from the days when he followed the Browns, then his favorite team.

Gary Pinkel, former Kent State teammate, said recently, "Jack Lambert stood out because of his competitiveness. He was the most competitive football player I've ever been around. It made him a great athlete and brought him much success." Pinkel now is the head football coach at the University of Toledo. A former All-M.A.C. first-team tight end, he was also an All-American honorable mention selection.

Then came that pro scout, an anonymous character who

appeared at a 1973 Kent game to observe Jack Lambert. After watching the game, he declared: "Jack Lambert will never play in the National Football League." Whoever he was, his rash judgment earned him a center seat in the House of Fools.

But Lambert persevered against the odds. He detoured around roadblocks and overcame adversities by believing in himself and making whatever sacrifices were necessary. A major sacrifice was giving up his academic classes. He didn't graduate from Kent State. Extensive weight training became top priority.

Coach James called the home office of the team that had sent the anonymous scout. "I told them I didn't think they would want to be represented by a guy who would say things like that. I said, 'This is not fair to the players.' " He felt the criticism basically was about Jack's lack of weight.

All winter The Stork's work habits continued in the weight room... with a pause in January to watch Super Bowl VIII. Joining him at Kent State to view the telecast were some football buddies. A few years later, Lambert recalled:

"I remember sitting in my dorm the day of the 1974 Super Bowl and actually debating whether I should watch it or not. If anyone had told me then that I'd be the starting middle-linebacker on the winning Super Bowl team the next year, I'd a'told him to go chase himself.

"Don't get me wrong. I knew deep down inside that I could do it, that I was good, but nobody else much seemed to agree with me," he added.

Lambert was being no more than realistic to admit that his own inner convictions were not enough. Somebody else had to agree with him. Thousands of players have dreams of playing ball, but the percentages against them are staggering.

The road from the college football playing field to that of the NFL loomed long and difficult. Imagine there are 196 colleges in NCAA Division 1-A and 1-AA with major football programs, all of which are religiously scouted by the pros and the scouting combines. Each team has perhaps twenty-five certified starters—offense, defense, and specialty players like placekickers, punters, and kick returners. That turns out to be 4,900 college players who are looked at in a given year.

Of the 4,900, only about 400 will be invited to the NFL—Combine Camp at the RCA Dome in Indianapolis for close scrutiny by NFL teams. And only 360 will actually be drafted. ...In sum, that is about 7 percent of the 4,900 college starters who could conceivably harbor dreams of making it to the pros. The NFL is an exclusive club.

A player must have outstanding abilities in order even to be considered; otherwise his disappointments can be deep and permanent.

The Big Day finally came: NFL draft day, 1974. First picks came and went. Then came second-round picks. The Pittsburgh Steelers were undecided. Who should they draft? They stammered around with the idea of selecting Lambert; but his tall and rangy build didn't fit the standard concept of a pro middle-linebacker. Most men who play that position are shorter and built "stocky," averaging 240 lbs. Still, Pittsburgh's team of planners sensed that Lambert had "something special" — his intensity. They knew he was a man blessed with athletic ability and, most of all, "football sense." Time became a factor. The clock kept ticking. Down to the last five seconds of the round! — Pittsburgh had to make a choice! Pushed for time, the Steelers opted for Lambert. They determined they could use him somewhere, so Lambert became part of NFL football draft history. As future events would show, it was one of the "six best" drafts ever.

Of what are generally considered the six best drafts ever, the Bears own three. Three of the other drafts were turned in by the Green Bay Packers, the Pittsburgh Steelers, and the Dallas Cowboys. In 1958, Green Bay took two future Hall of Famers, linebacker Ray Nitschke and fullback Jim Taylor. In 1974, the Steelers took Hall of Fame middle-linebacker Jack Lambert, wide receivers Lynn Swann and John Stallworth, and center Mike Webster. In 1975, Dallas signed defensive tackle Randy White, linebacker Thomas "Hollywood" Henderson, linebacker Bob Breunig, guard Herbert Scott, running back Scott Laidlaw, and guard Burton Lawless.

Those last five seconds have proved crucial to Pittsburgh — known as a momentous period of time, etched in Steeler football history. Why? Because of those few ticks of the clock, Lambert became the final component of the "Steel Curtain" defense— maybe the best defense ever in pro football. With Lambert in that defense, Pittsburgh went on to capture four Super Bowl championships during the 1970's.

"We thought Jack was a lot like Ted Hendricks, an outside linebacker who played in the Pro Bowl," Dick Haley, Pittsburgh Director of Personnel, said later. "We knew Jack was undersized, but there was no question he was a football player. We felt he was good enough to overcome any weight disadvantage he might have. He had the intensity and instincts to play <u>somewhere</u>."

Even at that, the Steeler management didn't know what pinnacles Lambert would reach. But Lambert was determined to be an excellent pro "gladiator," as though he had engaged himself in a fight to the death—to excel at all costs. Like trained fighters we've seen, going beyond their limits in the ring.

Woody Widenhofer, Pittsburgh's linebacker coach, called Lambert to tell him the good news. In their conversation, Lambert got right down to business. He asked if he could come to Pittsburgh right away to study films. He wanted to learn Pittsburgh's defenses—all formations and sets.

After that, Lambert got up at 6 a.m. every weekend to make the drive to the Steel City. It meant a 2-1/2 hour jaunt from Kent, then watching about eight hours of film each trip. Coach Widenhofer was astounded. "Nothing like this ever happened to me before," Widenhofer said. "I don't think it ever happened here before. I figured he was either putting me on or else he had a great attitude."

"I guess I was just naive," mused Lambert a few years later. "I figured every rookie would be up there looking at films. I thought it was just plain logical." Jack's logic paid off in the years that followed with Pittsburgh.

A lot <u>can</u> be learned from films, at least most players and coaches think so. "I always studied films," said Raymond Berry, "to see the movements of the defensive backs. You'd be amazed at how much a film will tell you, if you know what to look for and how to exploit it. Some backs had their own trademarks...little things they did, things I'm sure they weren't even conscious of...like always beginning their back pedal on the same foot, or crossing their legs for a fraction of an instant, or always going up to block a pass with the same hand. If you knew these things, you could compose countermoves.

"When the season starts, it's a game every week and practice almost every day, and if the players don't know how to play their positions by then, either they won't be on the team or the coach has made a terrible mistake."

There were those who didn't care for films, like Buddy Parker — who had a successful career as head coach of the Detroit Lions and Pittsburgh Steelers during the 1950's and 1960's.

Buddy simply didn't like films that much. "I know what we can do, and if we find a team that can't stop us, we'll probably win. But most teams are better than we are [in Pittsburgh], so driving myself crazy staring at films ain't gonna make much difference, is it?" Most other coaches, however, have made the study of films an obsession. To paraphrase Karl Marx, "Game films are the opiate of the coaches."

Parker once made dubious NFL history when he challenged the famed quarterback Bobby Layne to a drinking duel. Layne turned him down.

In 1973, the Steelers finished with a 10-4-0 record — a wild card spot in the Divisional play-offs. But in the first round, Oakland whipped Pittsburgh 33-14. Something was lacking. Inspiration?

Pittsburgh had an outstanding defensive unit. With seasoned veterans like L.C. Greenwood, "Mean Joe" Greene, Dwight White, Jack Ham, Andy Russell, Mike Wagner, and Henry Davis, the Steelers had a powerful squad. With all that strength, the fans thought that Steeler defenses could—or should—hold back a herd of wild elephants, even more so the Raiders — yet they seemed to lack a final "spark" — the motivation to win.

Remembering those days Andy Russell recently recalled that

as an 11-year veteran, he really didn't have time to worry about a rookie player. He was gung-ho on playing every year to the best of his ability and had his own problems. Eventually, he claimed he got playing "out of his system." Today he doesn't miss the game. He never had any interest in coaching. Instead he is a Pittsburgh businessman and finds the business world more rewarding than professional sports. At first, he seemed easy to talk with, but later declined to be interviewed, saying he thought he would honor Jack Lambert's wishes "for privacy."

After viewing all the films, however, Lambert believed playing outside linebacker was not possible for him. Ham and Russell were too good. After watching Davis, Jack decided he probably could play middle-linebacker.

"I didn't feel I was big enough for the middle, and from watching films I knew I couldn't beat out Ham or Russell on the outside. But after watching the middle-linebacker (Henry Davis) on film, I felt I could play just as well as he did. I mentioned it to Coach Widenhofer, and he assured me I would get a trial at both the middle and outside."

At one point, Jack thought at best he would be on one of Pittsburgh's specialty teams. But he was going to "give it his best shot." In practice or in a game, he made a personal commitment to give it his all — a 110% hitter. Nobody could ever say that he did less than the best he could.

To add a bit more insight into what kind of personality he had we can portray Jack Lambert with a new term, the compound adjective, "need-achiever" — drawing a more precise picture of the future star. What does "need-achiever" mean?

Most students of human behavior hold with this basic definition: need-achievers set their own challenges or goals. They figure out that <u>one something</u> they want to accomplish more than anything else. Accomplishing that one goal gives them incredible satisfaction. Actually, it fills them with <u>ebullience</u> — high-spirited enthusiasm.

There's only one <u>proviso</u>: the need-achiever is unusually realistic. He will set limitations. He will set goals that he <u>knows can be reached</u>. Going beyond limitations to unattainable goals would be a "no-no." Failure would deflate the ego; so, the need-achiever thinks things out carefully and as thoroughly as possible. This kind of person is smart in knowing <u>what</u> to aim for, <u>what</u> is achievable — and <u>how</u> to do it. For Lambert, the goal he could set for himself would be the middle-linebacker slot. <u>Not</u> one of the outside-linebacker slots. The need-to-achieve is a powerful internal force, and the concept would define Lambert even today. It's not an "on-again-off-again" characteristic.

Lambert also became known for being fast, quick, and intelligent, a linebacker with good range. At first, though, pass coverage gave him problems. So he concentrated on Pittsburgh's defensive complexities and the territory to be covered. A voracious student of defenses, he developed all the speed and quickness he needed. Those were things he concentrated on every day. He continued pumping iron until training camp began that summer. Like Deacon Jones (former LA Rams d.e.) once said: "You don't get anything in life without working and sacrificing and suffering for it."

Lambert had known that fact somehow ever since childhood: the internal need to achieve a goal, and the effort needed to achieve it.

What events took place that helped Lambert become Pittsburgh's man in the middle? Did Jack become the inspirational "spark" for Pittsburgh's 1974 championship? Was he a team leader?

CHAPTER V

THE PATH TO GLORY

DON'T CALL IT LUCK

The path to glory is hard to pinpoint. To find it, people have to spend an enormous effort on a continuous basis. <u>Consistency</u> is the name of the game. If you someday want to join those elite who've risen to levels of "glory," remember: consistency applies to all fields of endeavor.

There's something else: <u>circumstances</u>. The situation has to be just right. Bill Walsh used to take specific World War II battles to make points clear to his players, the Battle of Midway for example. Let's take another example.

During World War II, General Dwight D. Eisenhower was Supreme Commander of the Allied Forces in Europe, a great general. Also — and not incidentally — a former West Point football player. He always put forth a tremendous effort when planning military strategy. Especially when he planned the cross-channel invasion of France, "D-Day." He had planned the invasion "go ahead" for a few days earlier, but the situation wasn't right. The weather was inclement: a severe storm developed, rain pouring down in torrents, blowing winds, with high waves on the English Channel.

General "Ike" was undecided — Go or No Go? He chose not to go, a monumental decision — then the weather cleared and the circumstances were right. Early one morning (June 6, 1944), "Ike" gave the "go ahead" command to invade, and the Allied Forces put out their best effort, making a successful landing on the Normandy beaches. As the Allies began to push the German army back — with consistent effort in the right circumstances — they found the path to military glory.

In pro football the same progression of events applied to Jack Lambert. Aware of what was necessary, he reported to the Pittsburgh Steelers' training camp his rookie season, planning to win a starting position. He had some things working in his favor other than his aggressive, intense style of play — more than his hard work, ability, and intelligence. Let's call them "circumstances" — being at the right place at the right time.

The players went on strike in 1974 leaving only six veteran linebackers in camp at Latrobe, Pennsylvania. *So?* Jack received extra individual attention from the coaches. Also, Henry Davis, Pittsburgh's first-string middle-linebacker missed most of the pre-season games.

Lambert made a few pre-season starts as outside linebacker where he didn't fare too well, but he showed a good attitude. After the strike, Ham and Russell layed claim to the outside positions so Jack moved back to the middle.

Then fate stepped in. Like Eisenhower's weather, it radically changed the situation. Davis returned to camp only to sustain a concussion and neck injury in the third exhibition game. His wife became ill at about the same time. Henry was put on the injured list, and he took time off to attend to his wife's illness.

Lambert took advantage of his opportunities. With brilliant play, Jack soared to popularity and became Pittsburgh's "man in the middle," permanently taking the position away from Davis. He felt a sense of accomplishment, beating out the seven-year veteran. But he had applied consistent effort in preparation, and all the circumstances were just right.

"Henry was always nice to me the few times I saw him," Lambert said later. "He helped me, taught me a few things. But this is a professional game you play to win at all levels. There's no room here for easy sentimentality. Either you play or don't play. And I wanted to play."

He was right. Either you play or you don't. Pro football was and is a business. Somebody will fill that slot — you or somebody else. Nobody should wonder then whether or not football players strive for what we're calling for lack of a better word "glory." <u>Somebody</u> will have a chance to catch that brass ring.

Football players are put on a pedestal beginning in high school and through college, especially the "stars" of a team. The system conditions them to be looked-up to as persons of distinction. They become popular — popularity and quick recognition become part of their lives, part of their blood, so to speak. Even though they might be humble about their status or fame at first, players find popularity and publicity are strong narcotics. Many find them addictive.

How does it work? The system starts early—with coaches, teammates, schoolmates, fans, and booster clubs in the local communities. Sports banquets and awards ceremonies —trophies for bookshelves and plaques for the walls — add to what seems to be evidence of glory's reality. Most of all, the <u>media</u> builds up players with weekly, often daily congratulations and hype.

In high school, Lambert was a favorite in a local paper, the <u>Record Courier</u>. Sportswriter Harry DeVault recognized Lambert as a rugged defensive back and praised him (in print) for leading Crestwood in most of its stats. Every week, Lambert was Crestwood's "top gun." To interest his readers and because the action made for good sports journalism, DeVault carried Jack to the pinnacle of such glory as was available to high school students at that time. He still admires Lambert and considers him a friend. Readers of local sports journalism began to aggrandize Lambert for his achievements, as they do for any outstanding youngster.

What does it <u>do to</u> a player... any player? It gives him a heroic feeling. It inflates his ego. Develops pride in his achievements being publicized.

Kids think they're invincible. They're popular. They're in very hot demand, like a hot rock group. No matter what they do, it's a hit. Everything they do is right.

Another way to think is that, because of all the publicity and almost instant celebrity status, many ball players never have to "grow up." In another context, John Madden expressed it this way:

"As a coach, the class that helped me the most was child psychology. I learned that, as a group, football players react like children. If you [were to] take any player out of the group, he wouldn't be bothered by the things that bother the group.

"Some go from high school to college to the pros and never are <u>forced</u> to think past the end of the season. The smart ones do. Many don't. They play their three and a half or however many years, but fail to make wise investments. Or get fleeced by... somebody. They end their years bitter, <u>frequently crippled</u>, disillusioned men. Dozens of former players swear, if they had it to do all over again, they would <u>not</u> play football at all. Biletnikoff was right:

"Anybody who says he doesn't do it for the money is full of bunk." Frank Gifford was right, too, when he said, "Pro football is kind of like nuclear warfare. There are no winners, only survivors." So much for that. It's partly what the players' union exists for.

<u>To regroup</u>: in an earlier chapter, we noted what need-achievers set goals <u>for</u>. They set one goal and achieve it for the <u>rewards</u>, the <u>feedback</u>. Public praise and publicity are heady rewards. After playing middle-linebacker in college, Lambert liked that position above all others. It became his favorite: his "position of all positions." Newspaper and university recognition was laudatory at Kent State, too. More positive feedback.

In his rookie year with the Steelers, when he got the chance to be Pittsburgh's "man-in-the-middle," he reached stardom. At least the <u>beginnings</u> of stardom. The "system" itself contributed to the first twinklings of glory.

AFTER ONE GOAL: WHAT COMES NEXT?

A truism in football is that the "defense wins games," and in pro football any middle-linebacker worth his salt becomes a national figure. Defenses are designed for the sole purpose of stopping an opposing team, and middle-linebackers gobble up a whole lot of the tackles involved. They form the corks in the opposition's bottle of fluid game plans. In the early days of pro football, nobody kept stats on solo or assisted tackles, but they do now.

Vince Lombardi once stated:

"The only true satisfaction a player receives is the satisfaction that comes from being part of a successful team, regardless of what his own personal ends are. More important, each man contributes to the spirit of the whole, and his spirit is the cohesive force which binds forty talented men into an indomitable force."

Playing was something Jack did well, although at first he had trouble with pass protection.

"Although I'm not the normal size middle-linebacker, I'm more suited there than outside," he said. "I'm much more at home there. My biggest problem so far is the many pass coverages, but I'm improving every game. I got my first two interceptions last week [at St. Louis], and that was a big thrill."

Lambert was ready and waiting for the regular season to start. In the opener, the Steelers shut out the Baltimore Colts 30-0. Jack single-handedly stopped a Colts' touchdown at the one. Good show. During the next two weeks, things went haywire. The Steelers allowed 52 points to opposing teams, and the man in the middle came under scrutiny. Sports media began to talk about the "undersized" middle-linebacker and how opposing teams were gaining yardage through the middle of Pittsburgh's defense.

But Lambert readjusted. He tallied a team-leading eight tackles in game #4 against Houston. Pittsburgh won 13-7. The next week, he caught two interceptions against Kansas City — plus he sacked the quarterback twice and recovered a fumble. His consistency paid off. He was again intense, with a nose for the football.

In the weeks to follow, the rangy linebacker's performance was outstanding at his position. His inspired play sparked Pittsburgh to a five-game winning spree, topping it off with a game-high 14 tackles in the Cleveland game.

The squad's enthusiasm carried the Steelers through a fine season. They finished the regular campaign with 10-3-1 at the top of the AFC's Central Division. Under Head Coach Chuck Noll, the Steeler defense executed remarkably well. Their players, snarling like a pack of rabid wolverines, rallied to be first in the NFL. They led the league in total defense, scoring defense, sacks, and take-aways! If you don't like wolverines, imagine a pack of Chinese bandits after a heist, counting their loot. The Steelers were exuberant! And Lambert — the ring leader — led the Steel Curtain in individual and total tackles. Back on the road to glory!

Next, Pittsburgh defeated the Buffalo Bills 32-14 in the Division play-offs. That win matched them against the Oakland Raiders in the AFC title game—with Oakland as the favorite under Head Coach John Madden.

During the week, Lambert spoke from his apartment while checking over Raider offenses that would be used on Sunday. He commented confidently, "I had to work to earn the position." He was sure Pittsburgh would take it all—even Super Bowl IX. "It has been a long season and I love being by the ocean, either water-skiing or just laying around the beach." He was so confident they would win that he planned a Florida vacation after the season.

The home team had a large crowd of supporters that Sunday, but no assistance. Sure enough, the Steelers bested the popular-choice Raiders 24-13 to take home the AFC championship. The Steeler defense claimed their part of the bragging rights. They attacked and contained the Oakland offense, an offense that had led the NFL in total points scored.

Linebackers Ham and Lambert led the way, each one making a pass interception. Ham picked off one of Ken Stabler's passes on the Oakland 33 and ran it all the way back to the 9-yard line. Pittsburgh's quarterback, Terry Bradshaw, capitalized on the opportunity. The Steelers moved the ball forward three yards, then Bradshaw threw a 6-yard touchdown pass to receiver Lynn Swann. The Pittsburgh crowd roared as the Steel City team held command of the game.

With the score at 17-10, Lambert made a crucial tackle on wide receiver Cliff Branch that prevented a tie. But the Raiders tightened the score to 17-13 with a Blanda field goal. Then Lambert picked off another Stabler pass. On Pittsburgh's possession, Franco Harris quickly galloped 22 yards for a touchdown. That ended the scoring. Final tally: 24-13.

Coach Madden summed up Raider feelings after the game, "It's really hard to come this far and lose." Coming from Madden, that's the understatement of the season.

A few days later, the United Press International (UPI), Pro Football Weekly, and Pro Football Writers selected Lambert on the All-NFL Rookie Team, and the Associated Press (AP) named Lambert the Defensive Rookie of the Year. Also the (AP) selected him for honorable mention of its All-AFC Team. Jack was on the trail to athletic glory!

Pittsburgh fans couldn't be contained. The whole country awaited the big day. In Super Bowl IX the Steelers were pitted against the Minnesota Vikings.

On To Bowl IX

In it's Super Bowl classic, the Steeler defense turned back the opposition once more. Joe Greene, L.C. Greenwood, Andy Russell, Jack (Hammer) Ham, and Jack Lambert — what talent Pittsburgh had. They were a mean "horde of hustling head hunters," out to capture a chunk of raw meat. That Steeler defense held the Vikings to a scoreless first half, and the offense held onto a narrow two-point advantage.

At the start of the second half, Minnesota's Bill Brown fumbled. Steeler fans roared as Marv Kellum recovered for Pittsburgh on the Vikings' 30. All right! The Steelers went to work on offense. Franco Harris capped the drive with a 9-yard sweep around left end, and the Steelers moved ahead 9-0. The Steel Curtain held the Vikes scoreless in the third period.

In the fourth quarter, Minnesota caused Pittsburgh hearts to race as they closed the score. They picked up six points on a blocked punt, with Terry Brown falling on the ball in the end zone. Their extra-point attempt failed. From that point on, the Steeler defense gave away NO points.

Pittsburgh took the offense. Talk about intense. They ended the scoring with a 65-yard drive, Bradshaw topped it off with a 4-yard touchdown toss to Larry Brown. Pittsburgh made the extra point and finished with a 16-6 triumph. Pittsburgh Steeler owner, Art Rooney, was ecstatic. After 42 frustrating years, he saw his dream come true: a pro football championship! The road to glory had been a slow, up-hill climb.

On the other hand, Lambert had accelerated to that same level. Before that season, he hadn't even dared <u>think</u> Super Bowl. He came away from Super Bowl IX <u>awed</u> at being the starting middleman for the champs. A meteoric rise to fame.

THE NEXT GOAL?

Lambert made remarkable progress in his second year. He set his sights high: All-Pro, regardless of past laurels. He hadn't been satisfied with his over-all performance. "There wasn't a single game in which I didn't make a number of glaring errors," he said. "In fact, there still isn't. What a real pro does is play without mistakes, no mistakes at all —that's what I'm shooting for." That's a pretty high goal for a need-achiever, but Lambert could maintain his focus on the final goal, who thought things out ahead of time to isolate what was and what wasn't achievable. No mistakes <u>at all?</u>

Although the youngest player on Pittsburgh's defense, Jack called defensive signals. He worked hand-in-hand with defensive coordinator Bud Carson. Carson sent the defense signs from the sideline, and the tall, lean linebacker went all out to polish his skills. At the same time, "Mean Joe" Greene took Jack under his wing. Jack was trying to cram all the football knowledge in his head as fast as he could. But Greene, a veteran, knew the ropes about defensive play and showed Lambert things that made learning easy. He did improve, especially on pass protection. His improvement helped stabilize Pittsburgh's straight 4-3 alignment.

"We got some 30 pass situations in which the linebackers provide coverage," he said. "That's a lot, but all three of us are fast and relatively light. And we got 'er done." The Steelers second line of defense was one of the lightest in the NFL: Lambert weighed 218, Ham 220, and Russell 214. Thinking about his own weight, Lambert figured, "I give away 20 pounds every time I step on the field. So I have to be 20 pounds more aggressive."

Even though Lambert was known for his aggressive, intense style, many football experts said Jack's <u>quickness</u> was the secret to his success. <u>Quickness</u>, they said, gave him the ability to make tackles from sideline to sideline — sort of like a Labrador retriever, back and forth from one side of a lake to the other to fetch the quarry.

Sam Huff turned "middle-linebacker" into a household word. Ray Nitschke left the image of a bone-smashing tackler. And Dick Butkus...? Butkus dismembered anybody carrying the pigskin. What a company of roustabouts: they cast the mold for a violent breed. Then along came Lambert—aggressive, emotional on the field. Sometimes he got "carried away" during a game and seemed cast from the same mold as his predecessors, yet Lambert saw himself differently from such stereotypes.

"I play the way that suits me best," he explained calmly. "I weigh about 218 while most of your middle-linebackers are 20 to 30 pounds heavier. Because of my size, I <u>have to be</u> active and aggressive, but that's as far as it goes. I tackle somebody as hard as I can and then get up and go back to the huddle. I'll play clean if you play clean.

"I try to get to the <u>football</u>—as opposed to the Butkus and Nitschke types who stood in the middle and dared you to knock them down," Lambert continued. "If I can run <u>around</u> a block and make the tackle, I'll do it."

Quiet and soft-spoken off the field, Lambert said he liked the outdoors: fishing, hunting, and boats. That's true because I've talked with the people he fished and hunted with. But on the field? Kenny Stabler of the Oakland Raiders described him this way:

"I liked to play against the Steelers because they were the best, winners of the last two Super Bowls. Their defense was a wild bunch, just like ours. I remember games we were winning when those guys would be fighting among themselves, arguing and cussing each other. It would look like they were about to come to blows. Joe Greene would be yelling at somebody, Jack

Lambert would be cutting up one of his teammates. They were emotional players, the best kind."

Now on to More Glory.

The Steelers looked impressive in their 37-0 trouncing of San Diego, their season opener. Then they lost their second game to the Buffalo Bills. Whoa! After that setback, they tore through the league with 11 straight wins, and Lambert was probably the main ingredient in the Steeler defense. Pittsburgh won back-to-back AFC championships — and another Super Bowl berth. Even without "Mean Joe" Greene for a while, the Steel Curtain stopped their foes every week.

On offense, the performances of Franco Harris, Terry Bradshaw, and Lynn Swann were almost incredible to see. With the help of a yeoman offensive line, ranked high in the AFC, Pittsburgh became the team to beat in the play-offs. They finished the regular season at 12-2-0.

A bitter 15° at Three Rivers Stadium, the temperature at the site for the AFC title game between Pittsburgh and Oakland. The stadium packed in 49,103 fans to watch the two powerhouse teams do battle on a frozen gridiron — almost an instant replay of the previous year. Like Bum Phillips said once after playing the Steelers on frozen turf, "There's no way to practice for a game like that, because there ain't no way to practice being miserable." It was cold.

Every game, has a hero. But who would have guessed Lambert as hero of the Oakland game? Anybody with football sense, but not before that game! During the action, linebacker Lambert recovered a play-off record three fumbles, and his defensive effort sparked his team to a 16-10 triumph over the Raiders.

Lambert battled so hard that his knuckles were swollen twice their normal size. His gold uniform pants were covered with blood. He sported two nice-sized welts across his face. Results were something like those from fighting a family of wildcats: a price for winning tough games.

"It's a great satisfaction beating Oakland," Lambert said

later. "Oakland is one of the best teams in pro football. You know you've played well when you can beat a team of that caliber." Even with battle fatigue, the middlebacker didn't seem bothered by the blood stains. "It's a tough game, a very tough game," he ended with a faint smile. "Bloodshed is a part of it. It doesn't hurt as much when you win." That day he must not have been hurting too much.

Super Bowl X — the Steelers Again — but This Time Against the Famed Dallas Cowboys!

During Super Bowl X in Miami, Lambert ran in stride with Cowboy Preston Pearson and knocked the ball away from Pearson's sure touchdown. The save helped preserve a Steeler victory. Then the game turned a little rough. Cowboys wide-receiver Golden Richards' ribs were cracked by a "sandwich tackle" between Steeler defenders Glen Edwards and Jack. Later Lambert threw Dallas safety Cliff Harris to the ground. Even when he was off the field, Lambert was still fuming about something.

Lambert was hopping on the sidelines like an animated pogo stick, huffing and puffing through his gapped front teeth, eyes rolling madly, exhorting his teammates on offense and howling invectives at the Cowboys.

Obviously, his emotions were running high.

The score was 15-10 in the fourth period. Bradshaw unloaded an awesome 59-yard touchdown aerial to Lynn Swan: 21-10. The Cowboys retaliated by driving 80 yards in five plays, and Cowboy quarterback Roger Staubach maneuvered a TD making the score 21-17 in favor of Pittsburgh. Not a comfortable lead! With 1 minute and 28 seconds remaining in the game, Dallas took possession — but failed to move the ball against the famous Steeler defense. The game ended. Pittsburgh had won its second straight Super Bowl, making them football's "glory team" of the '70's! After the game, the star middlebacker recalled the Harris incident:

"What happened was that our kicker, Roy Gerela, had missed a field goal and Harris came running up to him, clapped both hands on Roy's helmet and said, 'Nice going. That really helps us!' Well, we were getting intimidated there in the first half and, I mean, we are supposed to be the intimidators. We couldn't have that. So I just grabbed Harris by the pads and flung him down. After the game, the Cowboys said I was hitting late, taking cheap shots. That's bunk. That's sour grapes. I hit hard, all right, but I hit fair. That's the name of the game."

Later he added, "No one shed tears for Harris, either." Cliff Harris could attest to the truth of Lambert's philosophy: "If you have a chance to go for the interception or the hit, go for the hit. It makes a more lasting impression." Yes indeed.

On a personal note, John Pennell remembers:

"I used to go to Pittsburgh to see Jack play, and after the games we hit the bars. The table was always filled with no less than four or five free beers. We just couldn't drink them all! And the girls were crazy about Jack. They'd walk up to him and stuff their phone numbers in his shirt pocket. He had so many numbers he didn't know what to do with them all. I mean he had stacks of 'em. He'd throw them away. The thing was, Jack never wanted any distractions. That is what made him great: his focus with no distractions. He was the greatest against the pass — and I think playing quarterback like he did [in high school] gave him the ability to do it."

For Lambert — more honors. He led the Steelers in tackles and assists for the second straight year. Pro Football Writers, Pro Football Weekly and Football News selected him for the All-NFL first team. He made Sporting News, UPI and AP All-AFC first teams, and the AP selected him for their All-NFL second team. He played in that year's Pro Bowl for the first time: that had been his goal at the beginning of the year. His play was superb: intercepting a pass that first game. As a lightweight (for a middle-linebacker) all year at 220 pounds, his intensity and determination once again led him down that glimmering path toward fame.

CHAPTER VI

TEAM LEADER

THE MARK OF A TEAM LEADER

Lambert traveled to the Far East in the spring of 1976. Other NFL players went with him on the U.S.O.-sponsored trip to visit military bases. Jack discovered Hawaii and fell in love with the whole scene.

"Skin diving, fishing, boats...that's what I always dreamed of on the farm back in Ohio," he mused. "I've got to find me some place in the sun on the water." After growing up in those damp, cold Ohio winters just south of Lake Erie, he understandably loved the sun and easy life-style of Hawaii. Once he'd returned home, Jack decided to go back.

Why not? A bachelor with spare time and no family responsibilities, Jack became a knight of the road, living out of a suitcase. "I liked Hawaii so much," said Lambert, "that as soon as I came home, I flew back out there and stayed a whole month."

In addition to vacationing, the Steelers' middle-linebacker took up tennis that summer at the urging of teammate Jack Ham. They encountered one another at the Airport Racquet Club. "It's good for the legs, good for changing direction fast, and keeping your eye on the ball," quipped Lambert.

But the game had become more like kidding, especially when Lambert lost. After one workout, Ham laid it on thick: "You know what it was, Lambert? It was 6-0, 6-2. I won! You were never in it, Lambert!" Ham laughed and suggested a re-match on Friday.

"Great," countered Jack, breezy-like. "I'll get you then, you blankety-blank!" Both laughing, they walked toward their cars. Linebacker Lambert accordion-pleated himself into his red pearl Corvette and left the Racquet Club.

Vacations ended, and joking fell by the wayside. Lambert was ready mentally and physically to spark the Steelers on to victory when the next season began. Once again his determination blazed into fiery emotions in the locker room. It showed in his 110% dogged approach to practice. During games, he continued to intimidate offensive foes.

Just like when he was a kid, Lambert despised losing. Sometimes anger overwhelmed him at the very <u>thought</u> of being a loser. That must have been the case after Pittsburgh's fourth loss in five starts. A splendid October day became the low point of the season for Chuck Noll's squad. The Browns had edged the Steelers by an 18-16 score. The game had been a roughhouse affair all the way. Things worsened when Cleveland's Joe "Turkey" Jones upended the Steeler signal caller; quarterback Terry Bradshaw suffered a neck injury on the play. After the game between the two turnpike rivals, Pittsburgh's dressing room was quiet. Filled with gloom. Jack always defended his fellow players, and he was angry and unhappy about the afternoon. In that tense atmosphere, a reporter asked Jack if the free-wheeling hit on Bradshaw had been intentional.

"You take somebody and <u>smash</u> them upside down on the ground as hard as you can — that's not trying to hurt somebody? *Ask me some more silly questions, you jerk, and I'll give you some straight answers. Hell, yes that was intentional!*"

Having spoken out, and uncorking his bottled-up emotions, Jack complained about the referees, too. On that ill-fated day he said they made some bad calls. He stuck up for his team. Jack voiced what most of them were thinking but were not saying. His "speaking out" spelled leadership to the team, and it turned the team around. From losing, they turned 180° and became winners almost overnight. Like seasoned gamblers: losing it all, then winning big on the next bet.

Pittsburgh steamed through a nine-game winning streak

from that point forward. For Lambert — and for his teammates — the rest of the season meant No More High Jinx, and they racked up five shutouts. That locker room scene spelled courage and leadership to the whole team. He had the mark of a team leader. Lambert gained his teammates' respect as a player and leader by <u>doing</u>, not just by <u>telling</u>, and by speaking out when others remained silent.

LEADING ONE CALL AT A TIME

Football <u>is</u> played one play at a time. One quarter at a time. One game at a time. Players who think ahead of this sequence, lose their concentration. They begin to make mistakes — fumbles, broken plays, dumb penalties; the opposition will gain the advantage, control the game, and march down the field to a win. An excellent team leader won't let such insidious things happen.

It has happened in the past and it still happens today, sometimes at a steep price. A team will think ahead one game and lose the present one, setting themselves back in the ranks. Individual players often think ahead in quarters, in a period that's not going well, <u>giving up</u>. Saying to themselves, "We'll get 'em in the next quarter," losing their efficiency. Some players even think <u>play calls</u> ahead. They lose their train of thought in the present, adding to the mistakes of a mistake-ridden team.

A smart team captain <u>conditions</u> his team's thinking, <u>preaching</u> to them to focus on just the present week's game. And, on the field during the game, he <u>talks</u> to them about taking one play and one quarter at a time. Talks? He yells at 'em, every play if necessary. <u>Encouraging</u> individual players and the team into maximum effort for <u>this game</u>: the one right now. On the field, the defensive captain calls <u>his unit</u> to huddle, loud and clear so everyone can hear: "H-u-d-d-l-e — u-p!"

The defense assembles around its leader. As the in-play clock is ticking seconds down, the squad commander usually stands <u>in front</u> of his men, yelling out a defensive signal in a voice of authority. He'll have the glisten of alert enthusiasm in his eyes, no smiles — not even the ripple of a dimple. He knows <u>it's a</u>

serious game.

The captain hollers, "Break!" and all the players whoop and clap hands simultaneously, leaving the huddle for their positions at the line of scrimmage. A voice will be ringing in their ears: "Think about your job!" Concentrate on it right now! The team captain has not only the strength, courage, and confidence to lead his team, but also needs to be able to look <u>fear</u> in the face. All this is learned behavior from field experience. His teammates, coaches, fans, and even opposing teams admire the captain for his guts and leadership skills.

What <u>fear</u>? Fear of failure, fear of pain, fear of a powerful opposition, fear of the challenge of the game itself. Jack Lambert faced it all. Today his ex-teammate Rick Campbell always speaks of Lambert's fearless manner of taking on challenges. How he faced things "head on" — never taking a step backward.

During the season Lambert often appeared to be a wild man. As they always do, fans and sports journalists create images. They're good at it. If they could throw a little bawdy ditty in the game along with the images, they would. But teammate Andy Russell, an All-Pro veteran, disagreed with the image fans and journalists had created of Jack Lambert.

"We play a rather complex defense, and what impressed me from the first was that Jack just did not make errors. He never suffered from what you might call a 'paralysis of analysis.' What also impressed me that first year was the way he took over. We were a veteran defensive team, but he stepped in at his age and took command of the huddle like a seasoned player."

The "mean lean middleman" had another important attribute, too: his attitude. When someone says another person has an "attitude," they may be expressing a negative description. In the world of football, "attitude" has a slightly different color. When a player has a good "attitude," it usually means he's cooperative and positive about nearly everything. Lambert <u>loved</u> to play the game. When you love your work you perform better. That <u>attitude</u> made Lambert a pillar of strength, a solid leader.

"Inside, that's my type of football," he said. "It's like being a catcher in baseball. You're in the middle of everything... One of my strong points is getting to the ball. Outside you have to be more restrained. If a play develops inside, you have to worry about it coming back, a reverse or an end-around. When you're playing the middle, you go for the ball."

Off the field, Lambert usually was calm, quiet, almost gentle. At the same time, a gregarious sort of man. He was himself. He had yet another side: a lover of books and music. His reading tastes were fairly sophisticated: Joe Heller's <u>Something Happened</u> and Thoreau's <u>Walden</u>. Also works of John Updike and Franz Kafka.

But that on-the-field image was like a plague. It wouldn't go away. The media still painted him as mean, barbarous, wickedly ferocious. That image fenced him into a traditional mold — a form of folklore that spotlighted all middle-linebackers as the toughest of all players — even before television made "middle-linebacker" a household word. Lambert didn't feel right about the stereotype and voiced his disagreement vehemently.

"All you read about me is that I'm the meanest man in football," he objected. "Because of Nitschke and Butkus, the middle-linebacker has the reputation of being a wild man. I'm not mean. I play aggressive football. I can't say I enjoy hurting people. If I hit someone down there, I want to see him get up and <u>walk</u> off the field... People are going to write what they want to write, and I don't think I can do anything about it."

WHERE THERE'S SMOKE THERE'S...

Jack's media image had some basis according to one Mantua native who preferred to remain anonymous. Maybe Lambert developed a "mean disposition" from experiences when he was a kid. All signals indicate that sometimes he really <u>was</u> "Mean Smiling" Jack. "Jack had a mean streak that he used to his advantage," explained the speaker. "If he knew it would benefit him, he could be mean."

Gary Pinkel disagreed. "Jack Lambert is a down-to-earth person who would rather sit and drink a beer with a steel worker or some common folks than be in high society. He's not <u>mean</u>. Jack just loved to play football, that's all. He loved it."

Trying to justify (or cancel) this problem of "image," I've tried to find a linebacker like Lambert today's fans could relate to. The closest I've found is the Detroit Lions' Chris Spielman. Both men emerged from what I call the "Brown-Noll System" or influence in Northeastern Ohio. Chris played at Massillon's George Washington High School where Paul Brown played quarterback when he was in high school and which Brown established as a perennial football powerhouse as a coach. Chuck Noll played for the Cleveland Browns during the 1950's when Paul Brown coached them (as did Dante Lavelli). Some of Brown's coaching characteristics became a part of Noll: he carried them into his own coaching career. Lambert later played under the "Brown/Noll System" for the Steelers. A <u>Sport Magazine</u> feature story describes Spielman:

Though his athleticism is often under-estimated, Spielman's white-hot <u>need to win, dominate, succeed</u> is still the trait that defines him and lifts him above other NFL players...[my italics].

It might as well be describing Lambert. Spielman's statement about his coach, Wayne Fontes, is almost a word-for-word quotation from Jack Lambert when Lambert spoke of his relationship with Chuck Noll:

"Wayne and me have an interesting relationship — <u>he doesn't say much to me...He knows I'll do what I'm supposed to do</u>. If I'm not good at something, I'll triple up my work until I am." Spielman is now with the Buffalo Bills.

Paul Brown, Chuck Noll, Dante Lavelli, Jack Lambert, and now Chris Spielman...all from the same geographic region of Ohio. An interesting crew to think about, but our focus is on Lambert.

INFLUENCES ON THE NEXT GENERATION

An open question these days is whether collegiate or professional (maybe even high school) football does more good than harm to the majority of players. A few years ago, the publication of <u>Friday Night Lights</u> detailed how high school football dominated the life of a Southwest Texas community, and angry opinions flew back and forth from both sides of the issue. We all know fellows who will state firmly they could not have received an education if it had not been for football. They owe a great deal to football and acknowledge their debt freely. Coaches served as surrogate parents, guiding them in the right paths for their future careers.

<u>Some good points</u>. Football is one of the few places left in our society (Hall of Famer Don Maynard thinks it's the only place left in the public schools) that teaches discipline, and a disciplined person with strong personal commitment can achieve success in any endeavor. So they say. Football coached by the right kind of person can teach kids to believe in themselves and it builds self-confidence. Taught right, kids can learn to play "by the rules." Break the rules and you're out of the game, or maybe in the penitentiary. Those things stay with them over the years.

Does it build "character"? That's a question I've been asking for the past 30 years. Maybe character develops from being disciplined and from believing in one's self — but I have a tendency to believe that character is either innate or develops in early childhood, in the home.

I know and all ex-players know of quite a few coaches who exploit football players at all levels — from grade school and high school through college. It's no secret that some coaches encourage kids to put football ahead of their studies. We've all known youngsters who are football stars but who collect bad grades in high school and can't get into college — losing out on athletic scholarships. Some college players aren't academically inclined and shouldn't be in college in the first place. Somehow they were recruited to play — maybe illegally — their coaches managing to handle players' brush-ups with the law, keeping ineligible players on the roster. Dexter Manley's recent biography describes such a personal record. Those boys are highly exploited and usually become tragic academic statistics. They slip through the cracks — no education, no career, and no future. Head Coach Joe Paterno of Penn State claims that 50 percent or more of America's college football seniors do not graduate each year. That's a poor statistic!

Jack Lambert was one of such players at Kent State, yet he was able to defy all the risks and make it as a pro. Not many can do that — a low percentage. Lambert was also lucky that an injury didn't knock him out of the game in his first few college years. If it had, what would he have done? Time and money would have been wasted at Kent State University. So what kind of message did Lambert's record send to America's youth? It's ambivalent. At his football camps, he <u>talked</u> about the need to stay in school, but his <u>record</u> says, in essence, that athletes can neglect academic work, drop courses to stay eligible, play football, and go into the pro's. That's fine for the 7% out of 4,900 college players who make it into the pro ranks every year. But for the other 93% it can mean personal humiliation and shame, the pain of knowing they were living false dreams — and reality strikes.

How about the non-stars, the non-heroes of the game, those who played only in high school? Even linemen in the pros don't collect much glory, like the Redskins linemen who established their "Zero Club" with the motto: "One For All And All For Naught." The public forgets them. If the kids are realistic enough <u>not</u> to bank on football as their ticket to a career, many — even most — will lead successful lives. It's a crapshoot.

Lambert came off as "cocky" in football. "Cockiness" was an intimidating style he used on the football field, a survival technique against opposing teams, an attitude he learned in high school and he never lost it. Today it is a negative facet of his public life and personality.

We can almost hear him even now:

"You just don't understand. Playing cocky gave me the edge over an opponent. Those guys knew I wasn't afraid of them, that I wasn't a push-over. The same thing is true off the field, like being "on stage" with people you don't know. But with my friends, people I know…hey! That's only one part of me."

Somebody said that looking at people is like looking at a

prism: they look different from different facets, but that doesn't make any of the sides less real.

Football took its toll on Jack Lambert, along with pressures from the press, coaches, the games themselves — plus injuries and pain he sustained when playing. Jack always said that he never felt any pressure, but people who knew him saw the pressures. Recognizing all the things Lambert has faced in football and in public, it is amazing there are not more negative incidents to report about him — and other NFL players as well.

LEADERSHIP AFTER '76

The Steelers played with toughness and assurance in '76. The presence of their man in command of the Steel Curtain became a given. Football coaches say: "We are going to be as tough as our weakest link." We try to imagine a strong chain with one weak link, but with Lambert in the middle, Pittsburgh didn't have a weak spot.

Opposing teams felt his authority when he snarled and barked defensive signals through his gapped teeth. He spurred our teammates to victory, quivering and fluttering his arms and legs before the center snapped the ball. Always looking for the chance to pop a ball carrier with a crunching tackle. He represented the Steelers in the truest sense of that word, as the Pittsburgh defense helped its team to a 10-4-0 mark — to first place in the AFC's Central Division.

That year the Baltimore Colts paid special attention to Lambert. They faced Pittsburgh in its fifth straight play-off appearance and were especially aware of the Steelers' aggressive middleman on defense. Lambert had helped his team hold opponents to only 138 points all season.

"He's the best middle-linebacker in pro football," said Ted Marchibroda, Baltimore's head coach. "We may have underestimated him last year. There was Ham on one side and Russell on the other. So we tried to go after the young fellow in the middle."

But even though Baltimore paid attention, Lambert gave it his all and Pittsburgh routed the Colts 40-14 in the semi-final game. Yet they won it at a steep price. While throwing every-thing into the game, Pittsburgh suffered what could have been two lethal blows. Franco Harris and Rocky Blier — the Steeler's top running backs — were injured. Harris suffered injury to his ribs, and Blier to his toes. With Harris and Blier out for the AFC title game, the Steelers were left in dubious condition. In their third straight AFC title-game meeting, the Oakland Raiders found revenge, defeating the Steelers 24-7.

That year wasn't a total loss for Lambert. He was named the NFL's Defensive Player of the Year and, unanimously, cho-sen as All-Pro. His teammates chose him as their MVP. "There's no question in my mind that Jack will go down in history as the best who has ever played the position," Coach Woody Widenhofer said. Such a great year's ending for a team player and a team leader!

The 1977 season rolled around and the Steelers went to training camp without their "carnivorous, head-hunting" middle-linebacker. While his teammates were broiling in the hot sun, the '77 season was just two exhibition games away and Lam-bert was in Florida, a contract holdout.

Bucky Woy, Lambert's agent, insisted that Lambert get at least $200,000 a year while he negotiated a multi-year con-tract with Pittsburgh's management. *"Well, Bucky and me agreed I've proved myself these first three years with Pittsburgh and they should pay me what I'm really worth. You got a prob-lem with that?"* Finally, Woy and Steeler President Dan Rooney reached a verbal agreement. "I don't want to say too much be-cause he hasn't actually signed yet," said Rooney. "I think it's fair and equitable, but I also believe the same contract could have been signed in the off-season. I don't believe it had to take this long."

When all the suspense ended, his teammates applauded Jack's return—especially Joe Greene. "Beautiful!" said Greene. "I think a man deserves any blasted thing he or his representa-tive can negotiate. I am glad he is coming back on terms he can live with and evidently the Steelers can."

Coach Widenhofer was also pleased that Jack and management settled their differences...but he was cautious: "You have to be awfully careful. A player can think he's in good shape, but he can't be in football kind of shape after missing so many practices... He'll have to get into hitting condition by the league's opener. We'll have to see how it goes."

Jack Lambert returned for the '77 season, and what a defensive trio he anchored! Ernie Holmes and Joe Greene as defensive tackles, with Lambert in the middle. All three equally tough. Any two without the third would cause an ineffective defensive front: a defunct unit. They meshed together like the gears of a heavy-duty truck. Smooth, picking up power when shifting to a higher gear ratio.

Take "Mean Joe" Greene and Lambert. Joe was especially tough against the run. Joe didn't line up over the guard like most tackles do in the league. He was a little unusual, lining up at an angle between the guard and center. As a result, opposing teams had difficulty running either right or left. Although the blocking patterns of the guard and center looked simple, and though opposing coaches studied different ways to block, nothing worked against the Steel Curtain.

"And the reason was that Jack Lambert lined up at middle-linebacker behind Joe Greene," explained John Madden, former Oakland Raider head coach.

"If you tried to block Greene, you couldn't block Lambert, and if you tried to block Lambert, you couldn't block Greene. So you couldn't run to the right or to the left. And if you were passing, you had to use your right guard and center to block Greene. Whatever you did, it might work occasionally.

"They became the toughest gap-stack in the NFL, with Greene in the gap and Lambert stacked behind him. Pittsburgh was the only team that used it. Why? Mainly because other teams didn't have a Greene or a Lambert.

"All the talk about the Steel Curtain in those years, that was the Steel Curtain to me — Joe Greene in the gap, with Jack Lambert behind him," added Madden.

The formation is not what makes a defense great. It all comes down to defensive players chasing after the ball carrier, stopping up the alleyways and holes, giving him nowhere to run. Not giving him any daylight to run through. The word is "pursuit," and pursuit is what made the Steel Curtain outstanding. It was the secret of the Steeler defense, like policemen in hot pursuit of a traffic violator, chasing him at high speed. All good coaches teach defensive pursuit and gang tackling—from high school to college and in pro ball. It's the best way to stop an offense. Former Dallas Cowboy Bob Lilly spoke of pursuit during his playing days... and still does on occasion. He emphasized the fact that the more years the front four and the linebackers have together, the less likely there will be any holes. The offense's back will have to hunt for a hole — and when the back hunts for a hole, pursuit ought to catch him.

Lambert provided emotional glue that bonded the Steel Curtain together. His take-charge style earned him that coveted gesture of respect: the team named him their defensive captain that year.

In '77 the Steeler defense didn't quite reach its 1976 form. The Steel Curtain manhandled the San Francisco 49'ers' offense in the season opener in a shutout (27-0) in the year's first Monday night game. It was the Steeler's sixth shutout over their last 9 regular-season games and a credit to the defense.

During week #11, Pittsburgh took over first place in the AFC Central, with a 23-20 win over the New York Jets. In week #14, the Steelers rallied from behind to beat San Diego 10-9 and captured the AFC Central Division title. Yet they lost to the Denver Broncos in the division play-offs, 34-21. The season ground to a disappointing halt, because everybody in Pittsburgh had been thinking Super Bowl. *"Agh, don't even talk about it. I don't even want to think about it. I'll never be happy with this season — we're a better team than what the blasted records show. Shut up! Don't talk about it..."*

Pittsburgh has been traditionally a blue collar city, with steel production at its economic hub. People there make no bones about it: they are unpretentious, they have basic emotions, and they cherish the Steelers above all else. During his first years in pro football, Lynn Swann found the transition to Pittsburgh from Southern California required a period of adjustment:

"People in Pittsburgh are not flashy, [and] they're not out-going. They reflect the steel mills and the coal mines they work in. Millionaires in Pittsburgh never drive Rolls-Royces because they don't want the guys in the mills to see them living it up with the money those guys are making. In California, workers expect their bosses to drive flashy cars...[but] living in Pitts-burgh for three years, I found myself becoming more low-key."

Like everybody else, Lambert was disappointed with the season. He missed being selected on the All-Pro team. Missed it doubly because, with a knee injury, he had been forced to sit out three games. Still, Jack stood in first place with a lot of folks. The Cleveland Touchdown Club selected him as first re-cipient of their NFL Player of the Year Award. After all, he was practically a Cleveland "hometown boy." Right?

At that time, one of his teammates described Lambert as the fiercest of competitors. Teammate "Mean Joe" Greene said, "Lambert is so mean he hates himself!" That old image thing again.

Lambert seemed doomed to keep his unwanted stereo-type, his "mean" reputation. Yet he was determined to put his repu-tation to work in the next campaign. As defensive team cap-tain, he would get the Steel Curtain back in order and lead them from the steel city to another Super Bowl Championship.

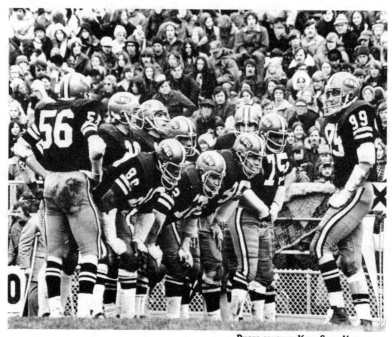

JACK LAMBERT #99
1972-'73 SEASON AT KSU

CHAPTER VII

CONTINUED SUCCESS

WHAT THE RECORD SHOWS

The Steelers continued their success through the 70's. They won two more back-to-back NFL championships and the classic events of Super Bowls XIII and XIV, giving them a total of four Super Bowls in all. As the first pro team in NFL history to do so, they reached a real measure of success. Yet Pittsburgh's progress didn't come overnight. Head Coach Chuck Noll did <u>not</u> win right from the "get go." He coached the team to a 1-13-0 mark in his first year, then finally captured a Central Division title in 1972 — something Pittsburgh had waited 40 years to achieve.

Club owner Art Rooney handed out cigars in the Pittsburgh dressing room after his Steelers, frustrated for 39 years, finally won their first NFL division title with a 24-2 victory over the San Diego Chargers. "It took a long time, but it was worth it," said Rooney, white-haired at age 71. "I'm not jumping up and down because that's not the way I am. But inside I'm bubbling like a volcano."

The Steeler defense won the game. They caused seven San Diego turnovers and held the Chargers back in their own territory, especially in the first half. They held Charger star runner Mike Garrett to only five yards rushing. But the San Diego defense was also full of fire. They made the Steeler offense spit and sputter at times like an old cold, armor-plated tank. Tackle Dave Costa led the Charger attack, with middle-linebacker Bob

Babich making a number of tackles. Costa was the one who sacked Steeler quarterback Bradshaw in the end zone for San Diego's only two points of the game. "I've seen and played against a lot of Steeler teams, and this is the best Pittsburgh team I've ever seen," said Harland Svare, the San Diego head coach.

The Cleveland Browns had defeated the New York Jets 26-10 that same day. It had been a must for the Steelers to beat the Chargers, to come out on top of the Browns in the AFC Central, then to gain home-field advantage over the Oakland Raiders in play-off action.

Starting from nearly ground zero, it had been a building process to develop Pittsburgh into a winner. What were some of the bottom-line factors that made it all possible? Our best answers came from some of the winners themselves.

"Chuck's a coach who commands respect. He treats his players like men, which means a great deal to us. He gives rookies a chance to show what they can do," Lambert said, looking back on his first year. "And there's the closeness of the team. We don't have the internal problems a lot of teams have. There's a mutual respect for each other. That's a nice atmosphere to work in."

The Steelers were "the real McCoy," the epitome of honesty and success. Team morale was high and that can be a prologue to victory. Houston Coach "Bum" Phillips once said, "Every team better have good morale. The team that feels like 'Boy, this is a great place to be' is the team that's gonna win."

1978. The Steeler offense was aggressive in 1978 with its emphasis on passing offense. Terry Bradshaw threw aerial strikes to Lynn Swann and John Stallworth—his favorite targets—all season. Swann caught 61 passes during the '78 campaign, averaging 14.4 yards per catch and 11 touchdowns. Together, the Steeler backfield and their skill position players collected most of the headlines. In football circles, these players are known as the "glamour guys," the spotlight players of the sport — the ones with the big smiles on their faces, something like Cheshire Cats, especially after touchdowns.

On the other hand, the Steeler defense was no slouch. They

were just a little older, with "Mean Joe" Greene and L.C. Green-wood at age 31. No less effective, still aggressive, mean and feared—just a little older. On the right side, Steve Furness was new at right tackle, with John Banaszak stepping in front of Dwight White at defensive end. At middle-linebacker, Lambert was one of the NFL's best. As the team's defensive captain, he was still the team leader, putting out total effort, always. Inspiring the team on to victory. Through his example, the "Steel Curtain" remained unified, worked hard together, and qualified as an "indomitable force."

The Steelers played like the Green Bay Packers under Lombardi, when it won three straight NFL titles in 1965, 1966, and 1967 plus the first two Super Bowls. Back then, the "Pack" could boast of a tough crew on defense: Henry Jordan, Ron Kostelnik, Dave Robinson, Lee Roy Caffey, Willie Davis, and Ray Nitschke. In Super Bowl I, Green Bay was the older, more experienced team — and at the half, Green Bay was ahead by only a 14-10 margin. What turned the game around for the Pack? <u>Defense</u> with blitzing linebackers. They played the second half with the instincts of ravenous tigers, holding Kansas City scoreless in the second half—to win 35-10. Still, the Pack paid the price for victory, both in hard work and injuries during the game.

Lambert had studied those games and realized the price for continued individual success—most of all for <u>team</u> success. Each week presented a new challenge. Each was tougher than similar weeks in the years before: it took continuous, exhausting hard work. It's always harder to stay or repeat as a champion than it is to become one the first time. Why? One big reason is that every team is out to get you, knock you off your perch.

A few years before, Vince Lombardi had stated, "To me, football is more than diagrams and techniques. .... You have to pay the price to win, and you have to pay the price to get to the point where success is possible. *Most important, you must pay the price to stay there.* Success is not a 'sometimes' thing. In other words, you don't do what is right once in a while, but all the time. Success is a habit. Winning is a habit. . . .Unfortunately, so is losing. . . .We have all watched people and teams achieve success—a promotion or a championship—and then be unable to repeat the next year. *Winning the first time is a lot easier than repeating as champions.*"

In '78 the Lambert-led, spirited Steeler defense had that singleness of purpose, that mental toughness needed to lead the AFC in rushing defense, giving up only 110.9 yards per game and allowing only 12 rushing touchdowns in 19 games. Each member of the gregarious Steel Curtain paid his price for victory. The whole team comprised winners, going 14-2 for the season and sweeping up the play-offs as well. *Winning* continued to exert an influence on Pittsburgh's success, bonding the team together. What was amazing: no histrionics were involved.

Some years later, John Madden commented on the "glue" that bonds successful individuals into winning teams.

"With a bad NFL team, I might have lasted two years and been fired, like so many other coaches. But when the Raiders kept winning, I kept coaching. And the more the Raiders won, the *closer* our team got. In any sport, success breeds togetherness. But don't be fooled, togetherness doesn't breed success," Madden said. "If a bad team tries to develop togetherness, that's nice; but it's still a bad team. Being together won't make a team."

Comebacks are hard to make, and the Steelers had a comeback in mind in '78, especially after their first-round play-off defeat to Denver the year before. The Steeler defense, harrying each opponent, was a big part of the turn- around. The rakish-looking Lambert was central to their trapping/confusing style of play. He and fellow teammates had an almost uncanny sense of knowing where the plays were headed, of how to stop their foes' forward movement, but Jack's aggressive style was still basic to him as a football player. He always had that weight disadvantage, so he always had to compensate by being aggressive, intense. Lambert couldn't have played any other way.

It was something he had to do, was driven to do.

"Every person has his own personality on the field," Lambert explained. "I've played aggressively since the first day I put on a football helmet. That's just my own style...I do some yelling and screaming out there, but that's just me. Jack Ham [Lambert's teammate at linebacker, 1971-1982] may have said only two words during a game, but he was one of the most intense players." Lambert hollered. Ham didn't.

Playing with "reckless abandon" is another way of putting it—throwing oneself into and diving into ball carriers. Anything to knock the enemy off his feet; allowing no time for buffoonery. Dick Butkus played middle-linebacker for the Chicago Bears. After his football days, Dick did beer commercials on TV. During those commercials, he was calm and cool. When playing football though, he was reckless almost to the point of being suicidal. Even with bad knees later in his career, Dick threw himself at an oncoming runner, or if need be dived into him. He'd bounce back up and do it all over again.

"Jack Lambert was almost as reckless, and at 6'5" and 220, he was taller and lighter. When he lined up behind Joe Greene, you seldom could block him on a running play. He was a great tackler, but he was so aggressive [that] sometimes you could fool him by faking a run up the middle. He'd step up, then you could bring your tight end in behind him for a pass," John Madden recalled later.

Right or wrong, whatever Lambert did was for the betterment of the Steel Curtain. For the success of his team, like Stephen Decatur's "my country, right or wrong." On occasion, Lambert may have felt a little silly, like an amateur, when his being overly-aggressive let a play slip by him. But it was all in the price he paid for victory: his quest to be the best. Eventually the price was worth it. The Steelers entered the post-season play-offs. Once again, they were favored to win it all. They did just that—won it all.

Bruce Ahrens of Mantua spoke of Jack not as a gambler but as a young businessman. We'd not be far off today to see pro football players as independent contractors. At least we probably *should* think of them that way, with the amounts of money they're paid in today's pro arena. In a competitive market, agents negotiate the best possible contract agreements with management, something like local firms in contract negotiations with workers' unions.

Many of today's players are business-oriented. Beginning with their early years, they learn to compete and gain success in a tough, competitive business. After winning their "market share," they apply the same principles they've learned over the years, looking out for their own and their teams' best interests. Attainment of Number One status in all categories is the goal — whether it's football, running a Fortune 500 company, or a small florist's business. More fame equals more money.

Lambert *was* certainly success oriented from his earliest years, even while working in his parents' florist business. Jack learned the ins and outs of running a small business there, especially how to compete and make a profit in a tight market. He had a bird's-eye view as the company's delivery man. He must have learned the county and the customer list very well while carrying plants and flowers to the customers. Ahrens remembers Jack as the "delivery man," transporting plants and flowers all around the county.

Lambert delivered the goods in the divisional play-offs, too. Pittsburgh trounced the Denver Broncos 33-10. Then Pittsburgh and Houston played for the AFC title. The Steelers had home-field advantage at Three Rivers Stadium, and the field wasn't in peak condition. Despite a cold 26°, a steady rain came down as Oilers' Head Coach Bum Phillips walked onto the field in cowboy boots and hat. Bum was no drugstore cowboy. A real honest-to-God cowpoke, that's how they dressed for bad weather.

Houston won the coin toss. That was about the only thing they won. The awesome Steel Curtain kept Houston's ace runner in check. Earl Campbell met the Steeler defense head-on, to no avail. The Curtain pinched and fenced him in. Charged up by Lambert, the defense threw Campbell for four losses and caused him to fumble twice. He hit a stone wall all day, averaging only 2.8 yards per carry on 22 tries. After he lost the rough-house fracas that day, wouldn't you think Campbell would consider another career? Why would anybody take all those hard knocks? The outstanding Steeler offense displayed great running and passing, thanks to the generalship of Terry Bradshaw and the elusive rambles of Franco Harris and Rocky Blier. Final score: Pittsburgh 34, Houston 5.

Later, Bum commented, "Ice and wet fields hurt Earl because he don't run straight up. Franco does, but Earl don't. When Earl turns a corner, his feet are out here and his shoulders are over there. He's leanin' all the time. You knew blasted well his feet were gonna go out from under him, which they did. It not only affects a man's runnin', but he's always afraid he's gonna slip." He certainly did.

How about Lambert? He didn't slip. He made the Pro Football News All-NFL first team, the NEA second team, the UPI, Pro Football Weekly and Sporting News All-AFC first team. *Plus* he was chosen to play in the Pro Bowl for the *fourth straight year.*

Super Bowl XIII presented Pittsburgh with a new challenge: their chance to become the first team to win a third Super Bowl! In that record-breaking event, Pittsburgh played Dallas in the Orange Bowl. Terry Bradshaw completed 17 of 30 passes for 318 yards, his best day of the year. Of those tosses, four went for touchdowns—two to John Stallworth, one to Rocky Blier, and a fourth to Lynn Swann. Franco Harris galloped 22 yards for Pittsburgh's fifth touchdown. The Steeler offense flat *bombed* the Cowboys' "Doomsday Defense." For Dallas, it was like being in a field of battle, hit by steady flights of bombers taking off from a nearby airstrip.

The Steel Curtain must have felt a few of the same traumas when Dallas quarterback Staubach threw three strikes for touchdowns. Staubach connected with Tony Hill, Billy Joe Dupree, and Butch Johnson for TDs. Linebacker Mike Hegman returned a 37-yard fumble for another Cowboy score, and field-goal kicker Septien added three more points on a 27-yard boot that ended the scoring. But all that wasn't enough for a Dallas win. The Steelers triumphed with a 35-31 victory. A close call, but the Steelers ended the campaign with continued success. Lambert did, too, with 12 tackles to lead both teams in the Super Bowl.

1979 was another outstanding year for Pittsburgh. A time of extended success for the tightly-knitted Steel City club, but evaluations of them ran the gamut from positive to negative. "Wild, aggressive, mean. All those adjectives describe the personality of the Pittsburgh Steelers."

How about Pittsburgh's coach's personality? Chuck Noll was a taciturn man with a natural bonhomie, but many football fans and "experts" saw him differently. "The adjectives most used for Noll are haughty...snappish...prim...arrogant...uptight...cold." Something like Paul Brown. Nobody denied that this was *part* of Noll's personality, but it didn't take into consideration that he was the Steelers' primary organizer and strategist, and strategy never was a personality contest. Especially during the glory years when Pittsburgh averaged 12 wins per season (including play-offs and Super Bowls).

Then how did Noll keep his team motivated? It became something of a difficulty after winning three Super Bowls. The famed Lombardi said it best: it's harder to keep a winner a champion than to make a loser a winner. How did Noll motivate the team?

"One year Chuck came up with '*Whatever* It Takes'," explained George Perles, Pittsburgh's defensive coordinator. "After that it was his talking about '*distractions*'." [He referred to the brawls with Oakland and Cincinnati, with their subsequent controversies.] "Now, right after we won our third Super Bowl, he comes up with '*We Haven't Reached Our Peak.*' That's gotta be inscribed on our rings. He's got the players talking about a fourth ring before we've enjoyed the third one."

Obviously Noll had considerable insight on how to rouse his men. His communiques had more impact than the vibes from a jungle drum, and he never let up on his theme of constant success. How about the players? After being motivated so intensely, what psychology did they contribute to the Steeler success? They were the ones who played the games on Sunday afternoons.

The linemen slugged it out in the pit, the area from tackle to tackle, while the backfield hammered out yardage. If the linemen didn't open the holes, the backs became punching bags. When the offense hit opposing linemen head-on, you could hear the pads crack—like the Dodge Ram commercial: two tough mountain goats battering their heads together. C-r-a-c-k!

Terry Bradshaw was the man the offense centered around, the Man-of-the-Hour. But greatness makes greatness just as money makes money. Bradshaw had a host of talented receivers to throw to: Lynn Swann, John Stallworth, Bennie Cunningham, Randy Grossman, Theo Bell, and Jim Smith. Bradshaw's offensive line was a unit of heroes, headed up by All-Pro strong-arm center Mike Webster, a master at blocking those quick nose guards and linebackers. On either side of Mike, the Steelers had left tackle John Kolb, guards Sam Davis and Gerry Mullins, and right tackles Ray Pinney and Larry Brown. The backfield was well-equipped with Franco Harris and Rocky Blier, plus backups Rick Moser and Jack Deloplaine.

Defense wins! Regardless of their offensive power, lots of coaches swear by this credo. It's nice to have both, and Pittsburgh did. A strong defense also scores points. All year the Steeler defense scored with a defensive efficiency average of 4.13. They were second best out of 28 NFL teams, behind Tampa Bay with a 3.89 average—so defense was a big part of Pittsburgh's success.

What makes an outstanding defense besides speed and player strength? Most football fans don't know, because it's not talked about by the media. The coaches and players know and emphasize this important facet of the game. It's called defensive pursuit, and you can't win without it. Former Dallas Cowboy defensive tackle Bob Lilly described the pursuit concept best. Lilly spoke from many years of playing experience.

> Lilly says the object of defense is to go after the ball carrier. To plug up holes in the line and force him outside where the pursuit will catch him. That's the secret to good defense.

> Pursuit takes a LOT of DESIRE. If you don't

excel at it, you shouldn't play. You don't just "work" on it: you PUSH yourself to do it, that's all! It's the difference between a great defensive team and a lousy one.

Lambert and Greene were in the middle of it all. The Steelers didn't go wrong. The top-chop Steel Curtain showed its strength against Houston in the second game of the season, shutting off the Oilers' star runner. Earl Campbell gained only a substandard 38 yards in 16 carries, while the vultures in the Steeler secondary ate up five interceptions. The mean monsters up front sacked quarterback Dan Pastorini *five times*. Awesome! That defense set the stage for the offense. The Bradshaw-led offense put 38 points on the scoreboard. Final tally: Steelers 38, Oilers 7.

Two weeks later when Pittsburgh played Baltimore, 14 players suffered injuries. Later, after the Steelers drove 84 yards in the last nine minutes to beat the Colts 17-13, Joe Greene bellowed, "The mark of this team is that we don't make it [injuries] an excuse!"

On any given day, a good team can be beat. That's what happened against Cincinnati. Pittsburgh lost seven fumbles to the underrated Bengals, handed them two interceptions, and lost 34-10. "It's too bad it wasn't raining," lamented Coach Noll. "Then we would have had an excuse." The Steelers had outrushed the Bengals 327 yards to 284, and at one point the Bengals trailed 3-0.

But improvement is the mark of a champion. Pittsburgh left its imprint on Kansas City in game #11, and the Steel Curtain closed once more against its competition in the Steelers' 30-3 win. Kansas City gained only 65 yards rushing and 62 through the air. In week #14, the Steelers exacted revenge on Cincinnati: they pounded the Bengals back by 37-17. And they defeated the Buffalo Bills 28-0 in the season finale. Thus, Pittsburgh with a 12-4 record clinched the Central Division title.

During the second play-off week, the Steel City team crushed Miami 34-14. Receiver John Stallworth caught six Bradshaw passes, sparking the offense. Where was the famous Steeler defense? You couldn't miss 'em. Everybody did his job. Each player was a pillar holding up its section of a structure. The Steel Curtain held the Dolphins to only 25 yards rushing and checked Miami's ace fullback, Larry Csonka. Dolphin quarterbacks Bob Griese and Don Strock just couldn't get their sputtering offense to catch fire. "They just dominated us," mourned Miami Coach Don Shula. "It's an indication of their strength."

The turning point came in the fourth quarter of the AFC championship game between Pittsburgh and Houston. Houston quarterback Pastorini had engineered a drive from the Oilers' 14 to the Steeler 6. On first down, Pastorini lobbed a pass to receiver Mike Renfro, but it sailed right over the fingertips of defender Ron Johnson. Renfro caught the ball in the corner of the end zone, with one foot in bounds close to the line. Side Judge Don Orr was right there, but he didn't make a call. "What the hell is it?" hollered Renfro. Tentatively they called "incomplete" as Orr looked to Field Judge Bill O'Brien for assistance, and the two officials decided to have a "pow-wow."

"Right then, I knew we were dead," declared Oilers' Coach Bum Phillips. "No way we're gonna come out on top in one of those huddle deals." Bum was right. The referees ruled the play an incomplete pass. No possession.

"Then why didn't the guy (Orr) signal incomplete right away?" Renfro argued. "I never juggled the ball. The officials just choked. I was begging them to look at a replay. If they're going to delay the game anyway, why not look at it?"

Houston had to settle for a field goal. It closed the gap to 17-13. Momentarily, they had a chance to tie the game. But on that day Bradshaw threw touchdown aerials to receivers Cunningham and Stallworth, Matt Bahr kicked two field goals, and Rocky Blier slammed over from the 4-yard line for a final Steeler score, bringing the game to a close. Pittsburgh won 27-13.

But controversy stirred in the Steelers' dressing room after the contest. "I feel like we've been cheated," Joe Greene complained. "People will be saying, 'Yes, the Pittsburgh Steelers won *but...*' I felt bad for Houston. I can't take any satisfaction from the call. You have 22 players out there waiting for a decision, and you don't get it."

Pittsburgh might have won anyway. Maybe the Steeler defense was tough as nails, and the Steel Curtain closed off Earl Campbell & Company by rushing men in the gaps alignment. They moved the strong-safety over the tight end and shut off Houston's outside game with their linebackers. Houston gained only a total of 24 yards rushing. In retrospect, Pastorini said, "I think we waited too long to start throwing."

FOURTH SUPER BOWL

Despite questions and quibbling, the Steelers had their chance to win a fourth Super Bowl. No other team up to that point had ever attempted such a record. They would match up against the NFC winners, the Los Angeles Rams. But the Rams didn't seem to be intimidated by the Steelers' advance publicity: they shut off the Steeler ground game and were fearless before the Steelers' passing attack.

The strength of the Los Angeles defense lay in veteran players: Jack Youngblood (DE), Larry Brooks (DT), Cody Jones (DT), and Fred Dryer (DE). They intercepted Bradshaw three times and sidelined star receiver Lynn Swann with a concussion, clobbered him on a 47-yard touchdown catch during the third period. Pittsburgh was trailing 19-17 early in the fourth quarter of Super Bowl XIV, and the freewheeling Steeler offense was third and 8 on their own 27.

Coach Chuck Noll ("He's the man; he does it all," Joe Greene said later) decided it was time for a different strategy. He sent in the code words for victory: "60 Prevent Slot, Hook and Go." The play was new to the Steelers who had never used it in a game before. Noll added the play earlier that week in practice, designing it to penetrate the Los Angeles double-coverage style of pass defense.

"In practice, we must have tried that play eight times and never completed it," John Stallworth marveled, and Bradshaw added, "I didn't like the call."

Receiver Jim Smith was in for Swann. He lined up wide

right. Stallworth was aligned in the slot next to Smith, and tight end Bennie Cunningham went wide left. Stallworth began a hook pattern toward the line. His movement pulled in both strong safety Dave Elmendorf and cornerback Rod Perry. Then Stallworth sprinted long, graceful as an antelope; Elmendorf lost his footing; nickel-back Eddie Brown didn't read his keys; and Bradshaw threw the ball over defender Perry's head. Bingo! Like the great athlete he was, John hauled in the ball for a 73-yard touchdown completion. Pittsburgh moved ahead 24-19.

Rams quarterback Vince Ferragamo tried to bring his team back, but the drive ended when Lambert intercepted a pass at Pittsburgh's 14 with 5:24 left to play. Earlier, "Mean Smiling Jack" had ranted and raved at his teammates: "The way we were playing, I was scared!" But after the game and during questions, Lambert had cooled off. "We fooled them. Our coverage was the reverse of what it usually is in that situation, and I was deeper than usual. I don't think Ferragamo ever saw me."

On Pittsburgh's following offensive series, Los Angeles didn't adjust its defense. "They were in the same coverage," Bradshaw said. "I couldn't believe it." He hit Stallworth as he sprinted from Pittsburgh's 33 on another "60 Prevent Slot, Hook and Go" pass and Stallworth broke loose to make the catch between Elmendorf and Perry. A phenomenal over-the-head grab from Pittsburgh's 33 for a 45-yard gain—then a pass-interference penalty on the play benefited the Steelers. With the ball resting on the Rams' 1-yard line, Franco Harris took the hand-off for his second touchdown. That ended the scoring. Pittsburgh won their fourth Super Bowl by a score of 31-19. What a way to make pro football history! Reviewing publications for that time (as we did), you'll find that Bradshaw received the game's MVP Award. Like the son of a Louisiana preacher (which he is), however, he was humble. He appreciated the award but thought Larry Anderson actually deserved it. Anderson had returned five kickoffs for a Super Bowl record 162 yards. "He gave us field position all game," remembered Bradshaw. Pittsburgh center Mike Webster thought Ferragamo was the better quarter-back. "Overall, he did the better job," he said. Wendall Tyler of the Rams was the game's leading rusher, gaining 60 yards on 17 tries, even though Lambert and other defensive players hit Tyler hard. Wendall had to leave the field five times with stomach pain. Lambert recorded 10 tackles and four assists on the day.

"They didn't out-play us," lamented Rams Coach Ray Malavasi. "We ran on them, we threw on them...they just got those big plays."

And that was the Super Bowl. Did Lambert enjoy continued success? Yes, as a team player, team leader, and team captain. For the second time, he was named the NFL's Defensive Player of the Year and was honored as the UPI AFC Defensive Player of the Year. He was a near-unanimous choice on the All-Pro first team, making the AP, NEA, and Pro Football Weekly All-NFL first teams and the UPI and Sporting News All-AFC first team. That's a pretty good performance for someone with a partially separated shoulder! Lambert had acquired the injury in practice early in the season, but he played in every game for the fifth time in six years.

Jack made the big plays all year and, in addition, he led the Steelers in tackles for the sixth straight year. In 10 out of 19 games, he racked up double figures in tackles. The Stork made 13 unassisted tackles in the Philadelphia game— a season high — and he was the leading NFL linebacker in interceptions (6). Let's add one more kudo: he was selected to play in that year's Pro Bowl. That kind of record makes what all the experts call "A living legend."

Chapter VIII
Steel Curtain Meltdown

Once a champion, always a champion, right? At least your team is *expected* to stay on top. You're expected to block, tackle, and run with the same old 110% desire. Your team is expected to win every game—at all costs. In the eyes of many fans, winning during the regular season isn't enough for an NFL team. Don't forget the play-offs! A team with a tradition of winning is supposed to win its division, then its conference, and the Super Bowl classic to boot—or at least *play* in the Super Bowl. How about them apples for openers...for pressure?

Expectations ran high for the Steelers in 1980. They were almost rubber-stamped as the first team to win five Super Bowls: a team that believed in its coach as a leader. Coach Noll kept his players concentrated on winning football games one at a time. But the Steelers seemed well-prepared in advance: they were the juggernaut of the NFL.

Despite the ages of some veteran players, Pittsburgh's depth was impressive. Coupled with new talent joining the club each year, team depth enabled them to handle many injuries from the previous season. At the same time, the younger players gained worthy game experience. Every position had a backup in reserve. It made for a belligerent training camp, junior players pressuring their seniors for starting positions. The Steelers maintained outstanding balance and versatility, capable of defeating an opponent either offensively or defensively.

In 1979 the Steeler offense led the NFL in scoring and yards gained. Their '79 yardage gained was the second highest *ever* in NFL records. On top of that, they finished second in rushing and passing, with the highest rushing average (4.6) and a fearsome passing assault that worried enemy defenders. The Pittsburgh defense had sent six starters to the Pro Bowl: first against the rush and fewest pass completions permitted in the League. The Steel Curtain also ranked third in quarterback sacks and pass interceptions in the AFC. Going into the 1980 campaign, they knew their schedule would be a factor — their opponents weren't considered overly tough or weak. The Steelers were a team that very seldom lost at home, but could lose on someone else's turf. They carried a 16-game winning streak at Three Rivers Stadium as they entered the season. With the best talent and one of football's best coaches, how could Pittsburgh go wrong? One other big advantage they had: Noll had built the powerhouse team from scratch and maintained a high record of winning against stiff competition. They were oozing with confidence.

A team can be on top of the heap one day and down the next. Things would soon change for the Steelers: unknown variables have a force of their own. Most people understand change from their life's experiences — the ups and downs of everyday existence. Anyone can be on top of his career, the place he's always wanted to be. Then one day without notice or forewarning, the bottom falls out and yesterday's big success takes a swan dive straight to the bottom of the heap. What to do? Without a wing or a prayer, most people start over.

Pittsburgh started the season with a bang. They routed the Houston Oilers 31-17 in the opener at home during a battle of equal forces. The score was deadlocked at 17 in the fourth quarter, just before the Steeler offense exploded with two touchdowns to triumph.

There's a saying among football coaches: "You win with people," meaning with talented players. A team can be talented one year, but not the next. Why not? Frequently, age creeps in as the culprit causing a decline in an athlete's ability. To stay successful, a coach must constantly evaluate and shuffle his personnel. The key is in knowing how to use the horses in the barn—the active players signed for the year. And the coach has to bring in new players to replace the aging: football is still a young man's game. In Football Mystique, Dave Klein describes the problem this way:

> "In many cases, the reputations earned by assistant coaches are from successful staffs' parallel reputations earned by superstar players from [other] successful teams. For instance, Jethro Pugh was hailed as a new star at defensive tackle when he joined the Dallas Cowboys. And he played like it. But he had the advantage of playing next to one of the all-time great defensive tackles, Bob Lilly. And as Lilly aged, slowed, and needed less attention, Pugh's efficiency began to decrease. Would Pugh have been an outstanding tackle on a mediocre team? Maybe not. But we will never know."

First Indications of Meltdown

Pittsburgh football fans expected a continued Steeler top performance in 1980, basing their judgments on previous winning seasons. Steeler's enthusiasts expected to go the whole nine yards straight into another Super Bowl. But soon they realized something was radically different from their expectations when the Steel City team dropped a second game to the Cincinnati Bengals in Three Rivers Stadium. Cincinnati had its first win at Pittsburgh in 10 years! This typically hard-fought 17-16 victory for the Bengals made Head Coach Forrest Gregg most pleased.

"If anybody would ask me, I would have to say this is my biggest win ever as a coach," he smiled after the game. "When you beat the Steelers twice, you're accomplishing something."

After the game, Noll was furious about his team's performance. "What it comes down to is that we played one quarter of football," Coach Noll snorted. Not smiling at all. "You don't win any games that way." Maybe the stoic coach should have thought earlier about player age. The Steeler defense had begun to slow down. According to expert observations, the Steel Curtain was in a pre-meltdown stage. Like iron when a blast furnace begins to melt down ore to produce pig iron.

No wonder. "Mean Joe" Greene, L.C. Greenwood, John Banaszak, Steve Furness, and Jack Ham averaged age 31: these boys were getting to be a little long in the tooth for football. A few weeks later, Pittsburgh once again found itself in the scoreboard loss column with a 27-26 loss to their arch rival, the Browns, in Cleveland Stadium. On another day in the season re-match, the Steelers did claim revenge. In a hotly contested battle, they bested the Browns 16-13 at Three Rivers. No big win! "Quarterback Brian Sipe played good enough for the Browns to win," Browns Coach Sam Rutigliano said afterward.

"They pressured us all day," Sipe admitted. "It was a struggle, because both times we scored required great catches...they blitzed better today and disguised themselves better than in our previous game." Sipe felt the brunt of a brawling Steeler defense. He respected Pittsburgh's secondary coverage and admired how Lambert handled his assignments. He knew firsthand how the Steeler middleman had motivated himself and his teammates.

The Cleveland paper admitted:

> "Credit, of course, must go to the Steeler defense, which played its best game in nearly two months. The difference, to a major degree, was the return of Jack Lambert.

> "He is so quick and reads plays so well, he compensates for breakdowns elsewhere. Also, he adds fire to his teammates that seemed to be lacking when he was on the sideline."

Never lacking in ability, the need-achiever had struck again. Lambert still controlled the tenacious Steeler defense which was naturally easy for him—serving as unit-captain, calling signals, and leading the way by example. His vim and vinegar gave him confidence for the task. That confidence inspired his teammates. He wanted to control his own destiny as well as the team's: that measure of control satisfied his ego, and need achievers feel gratified in leadership roles. At the same time, Lambert personified aplomb and responsibility as a team leader. As the old song says, it's "nice work if you can get it," because it develops a symbiotic win-win situation. Everybody benefits.

Whatever the situation, Jack's personality adjusted to fit the called-for mold. He provided the spark that boosted the Steel Curtain's efficiency by lighting a fire under his teammates' rear ends. The heat got them moving. Some old time (traditional) coaches used to literally boot a player in the pants to motivate him, to energize a sluggish player into action and possibly to victory. That kick in the caboose sure got attention. So did Lambert's sizzle.

Once Lambert lit the match that year, the sparks flew. Once again the wild Steeler defensive pack turned into an artillery battery, blowing craters in the opposition's offense. Some teams actually liked to play against that crazy Steeler defense. Kenny Stabler said he liked to play against them "because they were the best...a wild bunch, just like ours." In the aftermath, the Steeler defense stood proud amid the crowd's applause, and Lambert's fan club flew their "LAMBERT'S LUNATICS" banner in the end zone, rain or shine. A resilient bunch, they possessed such a talent for overcoming handicaps that they typified the words of the old Marine Corps motto: "Their uncommon valor was a common virtue."

HOMETOWN SPECIAL RECOGNITION

On another special occasion that year, Jack Lambert stood proud during a crowd's standing ovation. Thousands of people had come to cheer and offer laurels to their hometown hero. Friday night, October 10th, 1980, the citizens of Mantua laid their highest honors at his feet. Just before the annual homecoming game they dedicated Crestwood's high school stadium to him and changed its name to "Lambert Stadium."

At a school board meeting that year, Superintendent Dick Tormasi had proposed the field dedication to the board. Former school board president Bruce Ahrens recently recalled Tormasi's question: "What do you board members think about naming the school football stadium after Lambert?" All the members agreed. Ahrens says:

"It was a unanimous decision. We considered Jack a children's hero, with good ethics, devoted to hard work. A real good role model.

"He must have taken after his grandfather [C.H. 'Bus' Harper]," Ahrens continued. "He was a wonderful person. I remember when Mr. Harper hauled my cattle to the Portage County Fair when I was a kid in 4-H. And took other neighborhood kids along for free, whoever wanted to go. Grandfather Harper was always astounded over how much money his grandson made playing pro football. His being a dairy farmer, it was something he never could fathom."

The ceremony took place in the middle of the CHS band, the homecoming queen with all her attendants, the courts and floats. A Marine Corps Color Guard and Band marched into position for the flag raising. At 7:00 p.m. sharp, the band played the National Anthem and the Marine Color Guard raised the flag. All stood at attention, giving a hand salute, while one marine raised the flag real s-l-o-w. Once Old Glory was in place, the homecoming game was about to begin. Jack had only a few minutes to speak, but the game was delayed until he said what he wanted. Ahrens remembers how Jack spoke from the heart, reminiscing about his years in Mantua and Crestwood High — especially about those rock'em, sock'em Crestwood-Mogadore games. How he once helped turn the tide against one of those state-ranked Mogadore teams.

"This is a real big honor to me, and it means more to me than any of my Super Bowl rings," Ahrens remembers Lambert saying. "I've traveled all over the country, Southeast Asia and Europe," Lambert declared with a smile, "and there are no better people than right here in Mantua."

"Jack always supported Crestwood football and the boost-

92   TOUGH AS STEEL

ers' club. He always came back when he could to watch a game," Ahrens continued. "He well deserves everything, all the honors." According to Ahrens, Jack never forgot his high school teammates and coaches. Polite and unpretentious that evening as he paid homage to them — he declared he was grateful to the ones who helped pave his way to a successful pro career. He thanked his family and hometown for their moral support. "Lambert was calm and looked serious, and he was pleasant in greeting people with a smile." Ahrens smiled too, as he remembered.

Then Joe Skender, former boosters' club president, presented Jack with the dedication award: a plaque inscribed with the stadium dedication decree, on behalf of the boosters, the community, and the Board of Education.

"I was very impressed by Jack that night," Skender told me. "He was about the opposite of a hard-nosed football player. He was very much a gentleman, articulate, and presented a good image for children. Jack spoke as an educated role model, a very gracious individual.

"Whenever he was in Mantua, he always stopped at the local bars to say hello to everyone. He knew all the people and was always polite. Jack was always a good sportsman, too, and presented himself well by good play," Skender said, looking off in the distance, reflecting. "He conducted himself well, was very intense as a ball player, and he never took advantage of his fame for the sole purpose of making money. I respect him for that. I always remember Jack as a private person."

Ahrens remembered that dedication night as special for Jack's mother, too. "In remembrance of the occasion, Jack gave her a special gift. As I remember, it was a set of earrings or a necklace, and when he gave it to her, he said, 'I don't want you to forget this night!'" It was a special night for Ahrens, too. As Crestwood's Board of Education president, he got to read the official proclamation dedicating the stadium to Lambert.

Bruce Ahrens served on the Board eight years and spent

seven years as a member of the Portage County Vocational Board of Education. People speak of him as "a gentleman and a scholar at age 50 already." Thinking more about Jack Lambert and his career, Ahrens mentioned Jack's missing front teeth:

"Dr. Dan Grayson, a Mantua dentist, told the story better than me. Grayson was Lambert's dentist. The only part I can remember is that one night Jack knocked on the doctor's door, holding his front teeth in his hand! Can you imagine?"

When I called Dr. Grayson later for an interview, to learn *how* Lambert lost those front teeth, Grayson declined saying that it was privileged information between a doctor and patient. Ho hum. From an altogether different source (an ex-teammate) I heard that Lambert lost his teeth in high school basketball practice. He jumped up for a rebound and, as he came down with the ball, hit his mouth on teammate Steve Poling's head! Enough sportswriters and fans have mentioned Jack's "gap-toothed visage" over the years to make his missing teeth fairly famous. Wonder what happened to Steve Poling's head? Bet he's still got a scar!

Back to the dedication. At the end of the ceremony, Lambert concluded with words of wisdom for players of both teams. Reflecting a mature attitude toward the popularity and glamour of being a football hero, "Go out and play the very best and hardest you can ... and play by the rules," he said. "But most importantly, I want you to have fun. *That* is all this game was ever meant to be." A mob of kids at the dedication crowded their hero for his autograph.

Ahrens remembered, "I said to him, 'Gosh, it must get old, signing autographs all the time.' And he smiled and told me, 'When they want your autograph, it never gets old.'"

Mike Norman agreed recently with Ahrens. "I think Jack would make a good role model for kids," Norman was considering why:

"He never had any trouble in his pro career with drugs and stuff like that. He told me at the class reunion how much the game has changed. He didn't like the fact that players were joking around, playing cards on the way back from a road-trip loss. I think that kind of thing made him glad to get out of the game.

"Then too, Jack was always conservative, and he didn't waste his money. The first car he bought, right after he joined Pittsburgh, was an inexpensive Ford Falcon—when the other guys were buying more expensive-type cars."

He's right. That's a good kind of record for a role model. Question is: how many of today's kids will follow it?

Mike Norman played first string center on the same high school team as Jack Lambert, and Norman pulled some tough duty as Crestwood High's center. Today he's Chief Supervisor of the Kent State University Grounds & Maintenance Department. He was also in Jack's graduation class and, at their 15-year reunion, Norman got the honors of pulling some more tough duty:

"We wanted to pull a gag on Jack," Norman told me, "so I was elected to present Jack a gift we'd got him. It was a Cleveland Browns t-shirt with Brian Sipe's number on it."

Jack presumably went along with the joke and laughed "Just what I always wanted—a t-shirt with Brian Sipe's number on it!" The whole class joke referred to when Jack knocked Sipes for a loop on three different occasions—in the 1978, 1981, and 1983 Cleveland-Pittsburgh games.

"Jack was a hard hitter. He never took cheap shots and wasn't out to hurt anyone. He put a hard lick on Sipes with a forearm blow—but with no intention to hurt him," continued Norman.

"Jack was a good student, pretty intelligent. But you know, when we were at Kent State together, Jack made a comment to me one day. He said, 'I better make the pros, because I'll never graduate from this place!' "

Back to Pittsburgh. Going down the stretch, Pittsburgh lost three of its last five games: to Buffalo (28-13), to Houston (6-0), and to San Diego (26-17). They defeated Miami (23-10) and Kansas City (21-16) in Three Rivers Stadium—a familiar pattern. A disappointing season. Steeltown's team finished the year with 9-7-0 and failed to make the play-offs for the first time since 1972.

Lambert couldn't believe it. No playoffs? Incredulous! "Failure of the Steelers to repeat as Central Division Champions in 1980, or even to make the play-offs, surprised Lambert," according to Chuck Heaton. Judging Chuck Noll's mood, Jack knew changes in player personnel would be just around the corner. "Whatever the reason for the fall, Lambert believes the coming training camp at St. Vincent College in Latrobe, PA, will be different."

COPING WITH THE MELTDOWN

After the season, Chuck Noll took an objective look at his squad. As tactician, strategist, and organizer for the Steelers, he would have to make a personal assessment of the over-all picture. He would try to pick up the pieces and put the puzzle back together again. Engrossed with the problems, Noll usually had a stoic look about him, with calm, piercing eyes. Actually, he liked a challenge, knowing it brought out the best in him. Like some people, he worked better under pressure. But he was not interested in publicity: he remained reserved and quiet when questioned by the press.

> "Some of the [Pittsburgh] coaches have mentioned in the papers that they may have been sentimental last year for some of the guys who were around a long time, but who were not playing up to their ability," Lambert stated in an interview. "I expect it will be a wide-open type of affair this summer. If you don't perform, somebody else will be there."

Bill Walsh has also spoken about the problems of rebuilding a team:

> "Rebuilding a team also involves releasing vet-

eran players who have passed their prime,... The Pittsburgh Steelers are thought to have suffered because Chuck Noll stuck with his veteran stars when they should have been replaced. ... A coach has to be very strong in his player moves. If he becomes over-protective of a player's feelings or sentimentalizes his history with the team, he can damage the team over the long haul."

Fans saw the first signs that age had finally caught up with the Steel Curtain. Aging was a built-in blast furnace, and the process of the Steel Curtain's meltdown had begun. Nobody could afford much sentimentality about it (any more than they could afford tears when the steel mills closed in the '70's). Company officials restructured corporations, just like coaches and managers restructured football teams. The old blast furnaces were torn down or dismantled.

1980 had been a rough campaign, and most Steeler players were glad it was over, Lambert included. By coincidence, Jack had come to know Sam Rutigliano, Cleveland's coach, that year. They met on the day of the Pro Bowl. He probably knew Rutigliano a little better than he knew Chuck Noll. He liked Sam's personal qualities and his football theories, especially things Sam said for publication in the local papers — a real gentleman, with a lot of class. Tall, slender, dark and handsome, Rutigliano paced the sidelines during a tight game. A bit of a flashy dresser, he was always composed, never lost his cool or passed a rash judgment on one of his players. Nor on opposing players and teams either. If Sam didn't have anything nice to say about someone, he didn't say anything.

During all his days with Pittsburgh, Jack had never been close to Noll, even though he looked up to his coach because he'd built the championship Steelers. Lambert once remarked, "I don't think he's said seven or eight words to me since I've been here...I guess he knows I'm going to do the best I can for him every Sunday and that's all he asks...He just goes out and tells us to play the way we can," Lambert continued. "That rah-rah stuff is for high school and college." For whatever reasons,

Noll wasn't a "fiery pep talk" kind of coach. He didn't provide philosophical locker-room speeches, either.

But Lambert had sustained hopes of Pittsburgh's making the play-offs all the way up to the last game. Injuries had hurt the team. Almost every Steeler got hurt sometime during the season. Guys frequently were in such severe pain that only obstinate courage enabled them to play. Still some other players lost sight of their priorities. Off the field, they veered away from their original objectives.

ADMITTING WHAT'S THERE TO SEE

It must go with the turf. Can player success draw an individual off course? You bet. Off the field activities sometimes become more important than a career in football. Or the routine of the schedule will cause mental burn-out, and burn-out will deplete both energy and the ability to concentrate. People wondered if that's what happened to Terry Bradshaw. During the off-season Bradshaw was indecisive about returning to football. Caught in a web of misgivings about playing, he finally sought the help of advisors. Players trying to figure out Bradshaw caused further controversy. But Lambert summed up the situation very quickly, pragmatically: "Either Terry wants to play or he doesn't. If there are any misgivings about coming back, he should retire. If his heart is not in it, this [indecisiveness] could affect everybody."

At the end of that losing season, Jack retreated to his own personal "hidey-hole," the exclusive Pittsburgh suburb of Fox Chapel, where home values ranged upward to around $500,000 in the early 1980's — that's still pretty exclusive in most cities today. Nobody could miss his place marked by a black Cherokee jeep parked in the driveway. The residence had four bedrooms and a large recreation room in the basement, where he entertained guests and worked-out with weights during the off-season. The decor was that of a bachelor's personal office, with an assemblage of football memorabilia stored behind glass in large wood-frame cases. He'd saved a fair-sized mountain of things — dating back to high school, college, and his early pro football days. You name it, he had it: awards, helmets worn in special games, trophies and game balls from championship games. One particular football bears the inscription: "Super Bowl XIV, Lambert."

Lambert wasn't so averse to interviews then as he is today. Chuck Heaton managed to visit with him during the off-season following the 1980 losing streak. Dressed in blue jeans, a plaid flannel shirt, and high-top shoes, Lambert showed Heaton around the place—a picturesque location where he liked to bird watch and see his flowers grow. *Bird watch?* "Mostly it's just to get out in the country and get away from things," Lambert explained. "I often hunt or fish on Mondays after games, that is if I can get out of bed." Testimony to those interests lay in his fine gun collection and fishing gear. "I like to hunt and fish," Lambert remarked. "Back in Ohio, it was mostly rabbits, but now it's ducks, grouse and occasionally deer." He seemed to be especially fond of trout fishing in Pennsylvania's mountain streams. Later, when he took Heaton down to the rec room, he said, "This is where I have my parties. A lot of guys come out here a couple of times during the season. We've had a lot of fun."

For a fellow batching it, cooking is always a requirement, if not a problem. A grilled steak with a baked potato was Lambert's favorite meal — and he knew how to cook it. Just how was it, doing all this alone...? Probably a little boring, maybe a little lonesome. Jack had always been a loner—everybody who'd known him spoke of him as a "private person." But at this stage of his life, sure: Jack had thoughts about marriage. Someone to share the years with and raise a family. He smiled at the questions, "Yeah, I'd like to get married if you can find someone who'll marry me," he retorted. "I'm open to suggestions. I'd like to have a family. I like kids, but I'm not going to get married just for that. I have to find someone I can live with—and who can live with me."

What did he plan for the future? Staring out into the distance, he thought a bit: a coaching career was out of the question. The long, rigorous hours had no appeal over a lifetime. He'd also developed a definite distaste for viewing game films, and the current crop of prima donnas entering football didn't measure up to Lambert's private, personal standards.

What about a life of the intellect, teaching, maybe? Ever the pragmatist, Lambert had considered it, finally deciding it was all right in theory, but in practice it wouldn't achieve what he wanted out of life. Offhand, he'd thought about law enforcement. *Law enforcement?* It might be suited for him—and he might be suited for it. At least he'd thought about it. At the end of the day and evening, he admitted that *feelings* directed his life, just like they do for most human beings.

Jack Lambert in the early summer of 1981 was a quiet man with a conscience and some serious thoughts about the future, wanting to achieve his goals and ideal life-style. Regardless of how he was portrayed on the field — mean, vicious, wild, cold, or crazy — he was a man wanting to do good things for the world he lived in. During that summer, Lambert decided to organize two youth-football camps. One was located at Indiana State in Pennsylvania and the other at Mount Union College in Alliance, Ohio. He loved the kids and he was their hero—another win-win situation. Jack continued to manage the camps for the next 10 years. On his staff, Steeler teammates joined with him to teach the kids the proper fundamentals of football, and the training sessions were a positive influence in other ways as well.

> "I tell those kids it's important to find something they enjoy and work to be good at it. It doesn't have to be football. It can be anything. If it's football, I teach them the correct way to play the game. I also tell them they don't have to use steroids or look like Charles Atlas to be successful. For a while there, it seemed like cocaine and steroids were in vogue for football players. I want those kids to know that for every player who uses that garbage, there are hundreds who don't."

Jack Lambert was a walking, talking example of the fact that having a positive mental attitude is important in football. Being positive builds confidence. Confidence builds winning teams. Some players can prepare themselves and others need a coach's influence. Lambert was one of those who didn't need a coach to prepare him psychologically for battle on the gridiron. This bigger-than-life football player, even though he was something of an introvert, had the will power of a genuine *need-achiever*. Over the years, other NFL clubs may have judged him "mean and lean," but they respected what people called his "histrionics." Yes, histrionics: lots of people suspected that Jack had taken up *acting* on the field. These days we even hear TV commentators laughing at players who "play hurt," suggesting that they're putting on an "Oscar-award performance."

"From knowing Jack Lambert, I believe most of his wild antics on the field were an act, a put-on," Pat Hively said. "It was a macho image just to intimidate other players... other teams."

Pat Hively was probably more accurate than she knew in calling Lambert's antics an "act." Much of football is like the theatre: acting. Players' images are frequently distorted by the media for dramatic effect. It gets to the point where fans can easily confuse the players with their roles as professional athletes. Lambert was right — both in principle and in feeling misunderstood — when he objected to the stereotype he was given. The fact is that an actor is not the character he portrays:

Clint Eastwood is not "Dirty Harry."

Jessica Tandy is not "Miss Daisy."

Jack Lambert is not "Mean Smilin' Jack."

Back in Shakespeare's day, actors were called "players," but today the names have changed. Today football players are called "actors" — especially when radio and TV sportscasters suggest that players have given "academy award performances" in faking injuries.

Making Do With What's Left

After the air had cleared from rehashing the 1980 season, and after the off-season was over, the straightforward middlebacker set his sights on 1981. High spirited, he was filled with enthusiasm. He always enjoyed playing for Woody Widenhofer, Pittsburgh's defensive coach. Jack thought highly of Woody, not only as a coach but also as a person. Lambert admired his knowledge of the game and the way he handled people. He still loved the game. "I still love playing," declared Lambert. "As long as I feel that way and stay healthy, I want to play. My #1 objective is to get financially established. I have a season to go on my contract, and I figure I have one big [contract] left after that." So it was off to training camp once more. Something of a joy? Not hardly. Training camps are not supposed to be.

Example: Milt Moran played tight-end for the Cleveland Browns and dreaded those perennial training camps at Kent State University, especially in the final years of his career. At his last training camp, he told me he sang a little song: "This will be the last time. Oh, this will be the last time." Hmmm hmmm hmmm da da da: those words were music to his ears and an incentive to practice hard as he ran onto the field. Did anything like that go on with the Steelers? Nobody reported such goings-on, but the Pittsburgh offense in 1981 was antiquated. Bradshaw had reached age 33, Larry Brown 32, Randy Grossman 29, and Franco Harris 31. They had started to slow down. Was the defense in similar shape? They, too, were another year older and the veterans felt the pain. To anyone judging their performances, they showed more slow-down than ever before. The Steel Curtain was melting down faster and faster.

One particular player was in the melting pot: "Mean Joe" Greene. He'd earned his name legitimately by being mean in those early NFL years. As a rookie, Greene annihilated foes by making late hits, kicking and punching opponents—even spitting on them—quickly building a notorious reputation. Greene seemed to carry a low tolerance level for affronts throughout his career. One example of his behavior occurred in 1975 against the Cleveland Browns. Greene didn't like to be blocked.

"With evil in his heart, Greene attacked offensive guard Bob McKay in a way that would have horrified even the most crazed wrestling fan. Mean

TOUGH AS STEEL

Joe stomped on McKay and repeatedly kicked [him] in the groin...Finally, a gang of Browns wrestled Greene to the ground and thrashed him. For the kicking incident, Greene was ejected from the game."

Some of that stuff cost "Mean Joe" some stiff fines. Over the years, he paid out a great deal of money.

At the '81 training camp though, Joe Greene wasn't mean anymore. He had mellowed with age. When the season began he was riding the pine (the bench). It was tough on him mentally to sit out as a starter. He'd played first string for years, but Gary Dunn and Tom Beasley took over the defensive tackle positions. They made a strong duo, with Dunn rated as the top down-lineman.

As Greene's cohort, Lambert was still just as mean as he'd ever been. According to Joe Greene he was. Whenever asked who was the meanest Steeler, Greene always replied, "Lambert!" Jack was noted for his ferocious on-the-field antics. The sports media took careful note of his throwing, kneeing, punching, and sticking fingers in foes' faces. Lambert was still the hitter-of-hitters in the League, collecting 187 tackles and six interceptions over the year.

One problem: the harder Lambert hit, the worse things turned out. Pittsburgh lost its opener to Kansas City 37-33 and was defeated the next week by Miami 30-10, starting off on the wrong foot. Although the Steelers managed to win a share of their games, going 8-8 on the year, it wasn't good enough for Steeler customers. A second-place Central Division finish was disappointing for Coach Noll.

Noll's Steelers didn't suffer the embarrassments of the 1934 team, known in those days as the Pittsburgh Pirates. That year team owner Art Rooney made a wicked decision to dress the team in striped jerseys. They looked like escaped convicts from the state pen. "The uniforms were pretty bad," recalled Armond Niccolai, a tackle who wore the uniform. "But since we had to buy our own shoes, helmets, and pads, we were just thankful to have uniforms." They took a lot of razzing from their opponents.

The Pirates actually wanted to play in their skivvy shorts to avoid the heckling. "The other teams really got on us about our uniforms," he added. "They called us 'the chain gang' and 'jailbirds.'"

Because the uniforms embarrassed the Pirates, they were forgiven for their bad season which ended with a 2-10 record. The jailhouse uniforms disappeared. "Everyone was glad to see them go" declared Niccolai. The understatement of the year! Chuck Noll was probably just as glad to see the 1981 season go, sensing an omen of things to come. The changing of the guard was more inevitable than ever.

As a rookie, Jack Lambert had been the final link in construction of the Steel Curtain. At the end of his career, Joe Greene was the first link, the first piece of iron, to melt down. He retired at the end of the 1981 season, with more veteran players in line to follow in the next few years. The Steelers have never again resembled that team of the 1970s: America's team. How rough was it for Greene to retire? One of football's most articulate spokesmen, Bill Walsh, describes it this way:

> "Why is it so difficult for players to step away from football? We have to remind ourselves what this game has meant to them. They have given so much to it, and it's difficult for them to finally let go. Football has been the center of their lives, the basis of their existence. It has been the source of their satisfaction and gratification, and also the center of their social lives and day-to-day existence. The game is their very identity. It's what they live for. So, there's a real loss, a real grieving when they have to leave.

> "This shouldn't be surprising. Throughout their lives, these men have been recognized only for their athletic accomplishments, not for any other talents they may have. They naturally come to the conclusion that football is all they have to offer. When they are then deprived of that, they are at a distinct disadvantage. They haven't developed other

facets of their lives."

Yet as the meltdown got under way, Lambert remained indestructible as always, leading his defensive unit — win, lose, or draw, tackle after tackle. The mode of a classic need-achiever. Once more, Pittsburgh's stellar middle-linebacker was chosen for the PFWA, NEA, AP and SN All-Pro teams. Once again selected to play in the Pro Bowl.

PHOTO COURTESY KENT STATE UNIVERSITY

JACK LAMBERT #99

Chapter IX

Fading Ironman

As the Media Saw Him

A 57-day player's strike delayed the '82 season. Everyone's schedule settled back from 16 to nine weeks. Because old pro Terry Bradshaw was holding steady at quarterback, Pittsburgh would orient its offense toward passes. Pass completions wouldn't be much of a problem for Bradshaw. Excellent pass receivers like John Stallworth, Bennie Cunningham, Jim Smith, Lynn Swann, Calvin Sweeny, and Franco Harris made things easy. At least it made them *look* easy.

Pittsburgh's defense was another story. The process of the Steel Curtain's meltdown continued in training camp, and two worn-out long-time veterans, John Banaszak and L.C. Greenwood, both defensive ends, were released from the team. Looking into the past as veterans began leaving, Lambert spoke of the 1970's Steeler defense: "That was one of the best defenses in history. I'm not sure a defense like that can ever be assembled again." On the record, Pittsburgh rallied to capture their share of championships that proved the Steel Curtain's strength. "In my first two years, we won two Super Bowls," Lambert continued. "I sort of took those two for granted. I just thought that's the way the season's supposed to be. I didn't really realize that other players had been playing for a long time, and maybe it was more special to them...That's why our third Super Bowl win (35-31 over Dallas in Bowl game XIII) was the most gratifying to me. We hadn't been in it for two years, and I wanted to get back there again."

Even though Pittsburgh's team changed, Jack Lambert

stayed the same. Playing with his same old internal fire and toughness in the Steelers' machine, he remained their internal combustion engine—pounding its pistons fast and hard. Lambert adjusted well to change. Good people had come and gone since his rookie year, some even becoming close friends. It became a constant problem of mental realignment with the newcomers: getting used to their strong and weak points. Covering on plays for their lack of experience, or just being patient until they developed. Lambert carried a not-so-easy burden as the team's defensive leader, the defensive unit's captain.

Things were getting rougher on the field as Pittsburgh began to take its lumps in losses. How rough? Rolling along in 1982, the Seattle Seahawks handed Pittsburgh a shutout 16-0, and the Buffalo Bills clipped them 13-0 — mostly because of Pittsburgh's faulty offense. Bradshaw and the Steeler offense gained minus yardage against Buffalo on a very cold day. Terry admitted he didn't perform well in arctic weather conditions. "Thirteen points is not all that bad when you're on the field all day long," commented Lambert.

In December when it was time to play their closest rivals, the Cleveland Browns, Lambert remained a hill-to-climb for Cleveland's offense. Assistant sports editor of the Ravenna Record Courier Lynn Arnold recorded praises for Lambert even while noting the Steelers' diminished performance. Judging Lambert, Brian Sipe and Cleveland Coach Sam Rutigliano spoke of their high regard for him. "In all the games we've played against Pittsburgh, Lambert was always the guy stopping the long run or making the big play," Rutigliano said. Cleveland had only a 1-7 win-loss record against the Steelers before that game.

> "He is the guy who physically and mentally controls the defense. For my money, he's got to be one of the best because of what he's accomplished...He is the most intense player I've seen, but he is also very bright."

Lambert was smart, shrewd, and controlled on the field. When making a tackle, the snarling linebacker tried to avoid

TOUGH AS STEEL

those "unnecessary roughness" penalties. Shifted from middle-linebacker to inside linebacker in Pittsburgh's 3-4 defense, "Mean Smiling" Jack still collected a number of tackles. The transition from middle-linebacker had taken place because of player changes in Pittsburgh's front four. The new group didn't have the ability to rush the quarterback like the old bunch had in years past, especially with nearly all pro teams running more deep-pass patterns. Those changes almost eliminated the tight end from the field of play. "I have to play a little more controlled now," Lambert commented.

"In the 4-3, I could follow the ball. It was more suited to my style. I can honestly say I enjoyed it more...But we definitely play the 3-4 well. We've got some young players like [safety] Rick Woods and [linebacker] Mike Merriweather with a lot of potential. They just have to develop it."

During the previous year's game, Lambert had put the "kibosh" on Sipe, hitting him on the head and knocking him out. Officials ruled the hit an infraction and marked off yards against Pittsburgh. But Sipe felt no resentment toward the Ironman Steeler, or said he didn't. "Jack didn't think it was a late hit, and I agree. I doubt he was trying to knock me out. He just did what comes natural to disrupt the play." That would disrupt a play all right. So much for the previous year.

In that December 1982 game, the Browns squeaked by Pittsburgh with a 10-9 triumph. It was a jubilant time for the Browns, something they would always cherish, especially over their rival Pittsburgh!

Vince Lombardi once said of a game's outcome: "After the battle, one group savors victory, another lives in the bitterness of defeat. And there is no reason at all which is adequate for having lost. The winner...to the winner there is 100 percent laughter, 100 percent fun. And to the loser, the only thing left for him is 100 percent determination."

Can't you hear him? *"Yeah, yeah, Mr. Lombardi. But that's blasted cold comfort for the loser."* The Steelers practiced hard the two weeks before the Browns game. They were 100 percent determined to conquer the Browns this time. Lambert was growling and snarling in his eagerness to engage the enemy at Three Rivers Stadium. Three Rivers Stadium is located in a geographical quirk, the intersection/meeting of the Allegheny, Monongahela, and Ohio rivers. An architectural masterpiece, the stadium opened in 1970. Cleveland had yet to win there. "I've been here for nine years, and it's the same old story," Lambert mused. "It's the Browns against the Steelers, and there is no love lost between the two teams."

In Steeltown barrooms, Lambert was often called the "baddest mojo" in Steeler history — some fans thought possibly in the NFL. The League players who voted on the Pro Bowl selections recognized Jack's talents. Once the ballots were tabulated, Lambert was named to a starting position, his eighth straight appearance. He was still a need-achiever when the term extended to the Pro Bowl.

To digress just a moment: good people return their phone calls, and semi-retired Plain Dealer sports writer Chuck Heaton is good people. In 1993, Heaton was in his 50th year of covering football for The Plain Dealer. Each week he wrote a column about memorable moments from his years of covering football. Its heading reads, "CHUCK HEATON: BROWNS SCRAP-BOOK." On a cold, drab day in January, an aging voice on the phone acknowledged the name of Chuck Heaton.

"Did you call me? What can I help you with?" He could help by providing information about Jack Lambert. "Lambert was the best middle-linebacker I ever saw," said Heaton. "He was more consistent than any other individual who has played the position. His chemistry as a rookie blended well with the rest of the Steelers' defense. He added the final touch. The defense was superb, but Pittsburgh would have had a difficult time winning four Super Bowls without him. They probably wouldn't have won all four Super Bowls."

Heaton remembered Lambert's pass interception against the Los Angeles Rams in Super Bowl XIV. He also made reference to "Mean Joe" Greene with Lambert stacked behind him as the Steel Curtain defense. "Andy Russell, Jack Ham, and L.C. Greenwood were also very important to the Steel Curtain. Russell was just a shade below Ham and Lambert in stardom. He didn't have the same physical equipment as Ham and Lambert; Russell played a lot of years with Pittsburgh teams that were not so good in the earlier years of his career. John Madden over-exaggerated when he said Greene and Lambert by themselves were the Steel Curtain. But he always exaggerates things..." Actually, Madden never said Greene and Lambert were all the Steel Curtain: he just said they were what the Steel Curtain meant to *him*.

Other writers also remembered that interception of Ferragamo's pass. Here are two who made special mention of it as being the "turning point" of the game:

(1)

As Ferragamo dropped back to pass once again, it looked as if Ron Smith would be open for a short gainer. But Jack Lambert suddenly back pedaled right in front of Smith to pick off the pass.

"We were in reverse coverage," said Lambert. "We worked against that play all week. And the ball came where we expected it. I don't think Ferragamo ever saw me." Lambert's interception was the turning point of the game.

(2)

ALL-TIME SUPERBOWL TEAM

Middle-linebacker — Jack Lambert of the Pittsburgh Steelers. He made a crucial interception of a Vince Ferragamo pass in the last quarter of Super Bowl XIV.

Ferragamo faded back to pass. He fired deep. Linebacker Jack Lambert cut in front of the Ram receiver. He intercepted the pass at his own 14-yard line and returned it to the 30.

"It was the defensive play of the game," said Mean Joe Greene. "And Jack was the defensive player of the game." "I don't think Ferragamo ever saw me," said Lambert.

"I saw Lambert at the last second," said Ferragamo. The Lambert interception turned the game around.

Receiving bad press didn't always arouse Jack's emotions. On the contrary, media stereotypes didn't seem to worry him much. "That mean and nasty stuff is just an image the media has come up with," he grumbled. "The thing I'm concerned about is what my peers say. I admit that I get a little excited once in a while, but most competitors do." All during the 1982 campaign, Lambert still remained an outstanding linebacker, but he realized that he might have to hang up his cleats someday soon. "At the end of the season, I'll sit down and look at my performance and my physical condition, then make a decision," Jack said. "I thought ten years would be a good career. By the end of next season, I will have them in — everything after that will be gravy." He was right about 10 years being a good career. Average career-life for a pro football player these days is only 3-1/2 years. Some players think anything over 3-1/2 years is "gravy."

We've all heard it or said it, when somebody is taking it easy on the job: "Aw, he's just riding the gravy train." Or, "Hey, I'm on that old gravy train. All the way to Georgia to pick some a' them Georgia peaches."

Gravy train or not, in the second 1982 meeting between the turnpike rivals, Pittsburgh out-classed Cleveland with a 37-21 win. Adding to his numbers in tackles, Lambert remained Pittsburgh's defensive pillar of strength. Pittsburgh was the toughest team against the run, allowing only 84.7 yards per game. But they gave up 234.7 yards per game in the air, including 12 touchdowns during the season. Too much! Lambert led the team in tackles, racking up 77. That number helped the Steeltown team to a 6-3 win-loss record and a spot in the playoffs.

At the end of the regular season, the NFL conducted a 16-team post-season Super Bowl tournament. It included eight teams from each conference, seeded 1-8 on the basis of their season records. But the Steelers lost to the San Diego Chargers 31-28 in the first round of play-off action and that same year, linebacker Jack Ham retired from football because of injuries. Result: the bulk of the linebacking would be left to Lambert during the next year. Could the "Ironman" do it?

On to 1983. Lambert was now an "old man" in the NFL, even though he remained the heart of the Pittsburgh defense. Bumps and bruises no longer healed by Tuesday. They took through Friday. Those were signs of getting old and of his playing time's growing short. Shorter by the year, day, and minute. One day at age 31, the "Fading Ironman" realized he was one of the few original Steel Curtain members left of the gregarious group that squeezed and hemmed-in their foes. Other star players were fading away with Lambert, too, including cornerback Mel Blount and safety Donnie Shell who were becoming old and rusty, like worn out jalopies.

"It has been a fast 10 years," Lambert said in one interview. "I hope the next 10 don't go as fast as the last 10." Then he smiled, "It's tough, darned tough, to be considered an old man at 31."

Tom Melody, Akron Beacon Journal sportswriter, described Lambert's NFL status after an interview as that of a player older and wiser. Age brings experience, and experience brings wisdom. Take an old hoot owl sitting in a tree. The wise old owl. You can't shoot him out of his perch. He knows where you're at all the time, because his wisdom tells him. When you pull up that double-barrel shotgun to draw a bead on him, the old owl disappears, flapping his wings. By this stage of his career, Lambert was like the old owl: an experienced linebacker with wisdom — knowing each team's offensive attack strategy and counter attacking with force, stopping them, leading the rest of his Steeler defensive teammates. Carrying Pittsburgh for the first half of the season, the aging Steeler defense scored seven touchdowns in eight games. Coach Noll safeguarded the team in numbers by using more rushing linemen in the 3-4 defense and in the four-man pass-rushing alignment, thus freeing linebackers to cover passes. He built depth in player personnel, making frequent substitutions — and avoiding too many bumps and bruises for any single player.

A significant change developed in the Steeler linebackers. Still Pittsburgh's best, Lambert wasn't as dominant as he had been in the 4-3 defense. Eventually, older players wear out. Lambert hoped he could give it a couple of more years and etch his way into NFL football history without regrets.

"Miss it? I don't think so," Lambert told Tom Melody. "I have given my best. I will continue to give my best...and then I will leave with no regrets." Not that he anticipated a sudden retirement to a rocking chair because of the knee brace he wore on an injured knee. "I give it some thought from time to time, that's all," Lambert conceded. "I know that, after you have played ten years, you don't have much longer to go." One day, he wanted to leave the game with dignity and with self-respect. "I'd never want a coach to come to me and tell me it was time to quit," he added.

According to Lambert in that 1983 interview with Tom Melody, he wouldn't miss waking up to Monday morning bumps, bruises, and injuries, nor would he miss all the miscellaneous agony and pain. On days when no injuries occurred, it still took a day or two to recover from the knocking around. Just how would it be, waking up as an ordinary American? Lambert often wondered about that. Perhaps it would be a dream come true — something different to relish every morning.

"I went to an amusement park to do a commercial not long ago," Lambert volunteered, "and I began to think back to how long it had been since I'd been to such a place. I've thought about other things the years of pro football have brought, too. Years without privacy, years when I couldn't go to a hockey game, for example, unless I could hide out in somebody's loge. I'm tired of that sort of life, sick of it. From time to time, life without privacy gets to me.

"Sometimes I wonder if being a successful athlete is worth such a price. This has been the hardest thing for me to deal with. I cannot justify the conduct of some people toward athletes. If I have a hope and a prayer, it is that, when I'm finished with football, I will be treated as a common person."

If the common, ordinary guy spent some time in the limelight, he would begin to understand a pro-athlete's feelings, learn first-hand about people bugging the "star" all the time. It's a lot of hubbub and a hassle. At the same time, fans ultimately pay any celebrity's paycheck with their loyal purchase of season tickets and all the hubbub and hassle is one of the things athletes "sign on" for when they sign contracts in the NFL. Looks like a Mexican Stand-Off, a no-win situation.

John Pennell, Lambert's long-time friend, confirmed that problem for Lambert:

"Public life was too much for him, though. People pestered him too much for autographs. Always wanting something. One reason for not giving autographs: he was so focused on the game, he wanted to keep that 'bad guy' image in all football dealings. He's married now and fairly private, living like a typical farmer away from the glitter."

Chuck Heaton summed up some of Lambert's feelings after a personal interview: amid all the turmoil of stardom, Lambert often felt all alone. "Hammer is gone, and I really miss him." He was speaking of Jack Ham, his good friend and roommate on road trips. Ham along with Andy Russell, Pittsburgh's great outside linebackers, turned many a play in toward Lambert, helping make the irascible middlebacker the team's leading tackler many moons. But Russell retired at the end of the 1976 season after 13 outstanding years with Pittsburgh, and Jack Ham retired in 1982. Both of those fine Steeler linebackers, those who won in Super Bowls, were destined someday to be inducted into the Pro Football Hall of Fame.

Once Jack commented on Hall of Fame induction. "People have mentioned it to me lately," Jack admitted, adjusting the baseball cap he was wearing.

"It never has been my goal. In fact, I feel uncomfortable discussing it. The Hall of Fame to me is Jim Thorpe, Bronko Nagurski, Jim Brown, Sam Huff, and all the great players I've read about. No, I've never really thought about getting there."

Heaton noted that, whenever Jack retired, he would miss one aspect of training camp: his chats with Father Raymond, a monk at St. Vincent College. The old ascetic had an inspiring effect on the fierce fighting linebacker. "I met him my rookie year and have been seeing him ever since," said Lambert. "He must be close to 90 and is a wise, interesting person. His only possession is a color television set, and he loves to watch football. He sends me a note or a card after each of our games."

When Heaton questioned him on the subject of drug use in the NFL, Lambert told him, "I know it isn't a problem on this football team. If anyone is using anything, they don't do it around me. If they want to go that route, they are adults, but I'm sick of reading about it and talking about it. It's hard for me to believe this could be happening around the league."

Lambert was realistic about the length of his playing days. With a few years left in his contract, he would honor its fullest agreement. But if his playing ability diminished before his contract expired, he would exit the game, anything for the betterment of the team and himself. It wouldn't be like Jack to sit on the bench or work against unfavorable odds. Need-achiever Lambert would feel frivolous and frustrated in an inactive role. Warming the bench just wouldn't fit his personality.

Naturally, moving on to a new career would satisfy his need to achieve — accepting new challenges with the same perseverance that won him personal acclaim in football. "I hope I know when I should get out," he told Heaton. "Some players hang on too long, and it's embarrassing for them and the coaches. I'll stay as long as I can please the coaches and myself. I could be financially established in a couple of years and be able to do what I want to do," he claimed. "If you have to do something you don't enjoy, you can be miserable, and life is too short for that."

A country boy at heart, Lambert invested his money wisely in the purchase of a farm, locating himself geographically on the outskirts of Pittsburgh. The natural habitat there is blessed with clean lakes, plus good hunting and fishing, where Lambert could live like an ordinary person, seeking the private life he'd always hoped for, staying away from the public eye. Yet, a big change in life style.

At the same time, the Fading Ironman wanted to be remembered in a certain way: his way, to be chronicled as a legend in his own right. "I would like to be remembered as someone who played the best he could every week. I want to be remembered as a player who always gave his best." Lambert spoke as if he were fading out of football.

But not just yet! All during the 1983 season, the big linebacker laid siege on enemy teams, playing his best brand of ball, riding full-tilt against opposing ball carriers. In full stride, he was still pouncing on foes, stopping them short of their destination. Lambert was no Don Quixote, charging against impossible odds. Don Quixote was no need-achiever, either. Where Don Quixote was an idealist, living in the fantasy of what *ought* to be, Lambert was the prototype realist, living in the middle of what *is*.

Once again the NFL recognized Lambert as pro football's best middle-linebacker and selected him to play in the Pro Bowl for the ninth consecutive year, topping former teammate Jack Ham's record of eight in a row. Lambert was the epitome of the ideal defensive player and, for the fifth straight year, received more first-team All-NFL recognition ballots than any other linebacker. The AP, Pro Football Writers Association, Sports Illustrated, Sporting News, and Pro Football Weekly selected him for their teams. They rated him the Steelers' main luminary on defense and undisputed team leader. He earned that role with 159 tackles (91 solos), leading Pittsburgh in that department for the 10th straight time. He racked up four quarterback sacks and two fumble recoveries.

Lambert also received praise for his successful transition from the 4-3 defense to the 3-4 during the previous two seasons and for changing from middle-linebacker to inside linebacker, not an easy shift. He was outstanding on pass coverage, with pass interceptions against Cincinnati and Cleveland. He collected a career total of 28 steals to place fifth among all-time NFL linebackers. The leaders at the time were Don Shinnick (37), Stan White (34), Jack Ham (32), and Steve Nelson (30). Lambert also won the George Halas trophy, awarded each year to the NFL's outstanding defensive player. Famous for single-game tackling performances, he tabulated 10 or more tackles eight times, including 19 against the Minnesota Vikings and Cincinnati Bengals. He also made 13 tackles against the Raiders. That's an enormous number of tackles! Once again, Lambert's performance qualified him as a successful need-achiever in one of its rarest forms.

Lambert helped Pittsburgh to a 10-6 mark in 1983 and first place in the Central Division. But the Steelers lost in the divisional play-offs to the L.A. Raiders, 38-10. Pretty good effort for a so-called Fading Ironman, right? Fading... who's fading? Not Jack Lambert! He would be back again in 1984. That's how he had it figured. The media did, too.

CHAPTER X
FINAL INJURY

Tough as a piece of forged steel in a Pittsburgh steel mill, opposing teams will be foolish to try to cut through Lambert in the up and coming football season. And the boys will think twice about pulling any "folly" on Lambert at his sixth youth football summer camp in 1984. In part, he used the camp to prepare himself mentally for pro ball. Playing alongside 340 kids was enough to sharpen anybody's thinking.

"These kids get me ready for the season," Lambert told Tom Melody. "They get me to thinking about football again. I coach them—but, at the same time, I coach myself." Lambert always had a high tolerance for pain. His shin splints and banged-up thumbs were a bit of a nuisance, because he'd acquired shin splints from the hard surface on the camp's practice field. But the sore thumbs? "Carpenter's thumbs," he explained. "Maybe I'll get that house done some day," completing his dream of building a home in the Pennsylvania hills.

Young students of the game listened to the all-pro middle-linebacker's beliefs, an ironclad ideology that had brought fame and fortune to a need-achiever, and it gave them direction. For some it provided a purpose for their lives. Actually, Lambert was a teacher at heart, and the kids at football camp were all ears, soaking up his lessons. Could Jack have missed his real calling in life?

"I talk to them the way I once talked to my-self," he said. "I tell them to hustle, I tell them to battle for what they want, I tell them to make the most of what they have been given. I tell them, too, that if they do their best and then don't reach their goals, they have no reason for regret. They did their best and somebody else was better, that's all. Sooner or later, there'll always be somebody better."

Lambert wasn't always certain about his football ability, but he was always sure about how much he wanted to play, how bad he wanted to win. "I'd heard what some of these kids have heard or will hear," Lambert continued. "I'd heard that others were bigger, others were faster, others were better. Maybe they were, but none of them was going to work harder or try harder than I."

"Fear of failure probably motivated Lambert to success," said Joe Gordon. Joe is Director of Communications for the Pittsburgh Steelers, and recently he was thinking back when Lambert was on board. "Also, a desire to succeed prompted Jack. It showed in his behavior on road trips. On road trips, Lambert was quiet," Gordon reflected. "He kept to himself and spent time reading books. At home games, though, he was something of a practical joker in the locker room."

Actually, more than "fear" is involved for great players. John Madden underscored the subtle difference this way when he discussed the key qualities all great players have:

"*Pride.* People with pride make a commitment to be the best, to win all their games, to lead the league. For those people, fear of failure is the greatest motivator. Their pride pushes against that fear. Without pride, fear of failure is just fear."

After 10 years of pro football, making it big, Lambert had developed philosophical ideas and was engaged in the "art of wondering." Wondering about his contributions to society. Is there a reason to be here on God's green acres? Yes. What ... to leave something worthy to others? To impart ideas or some knowledge to society? Answers: yes and no.

Jack wasn't lavish in his lifestyle. He wasn't a penny-pincher or skinflint, but he lived pretty close to the vest. "He was just a conservative spender," Gordon said, "not spending a lot on clothes and other stuff."

"I think about teachers and I think about coaches: I think about all the good they do," Lambert was talking to Tom Melody early that summer. "What good do we, professional athletes, do? Maybe we bring some entertainment, some happiness, to others. I guess that's what we are, entertainers," he decided. He might have added they were role models. During those youth camps, Lambert was a football philosopher, instilling some values in the minds of at least a few of America's youngsters.

He never associated himself with peers who set bad examples, especially not with those using or selling drugs. "I pick up the paper and I read about this athlete or that athlete and his involvement with drugs.

"There's all the talk about pressure, about how the pressure of professional athletics causes these things to happen.

"Who buys that? I don't. If those so-called athletes want to know about pressure, they ought to talk to a laid-off steelworker with kids to feed. That's pressure."

According to Joe Gordon, Lambert didn't even lead a fast social life, let alone participate in all the other stuff some players get into. "I never knew of any girls chasing him — or him chasing any girls. I don't even know how he met his wife. I know she never worked for the Steelers, like a secretary or in ticket sales." What about the rumor of Lambert's going to bars and getting into fights, accounting for some of his "social activities"? "That just isn't true," Gordon insisted. "Jack never got into any bar fights when he was with Pittsburgh."

About those steelworkers and the pressure Lambert mentioned: in 1984, most of the steelworkers who were laid off never got their jobs back. The plants they worked in either closed or cut their work forces drastically. True not only in Pittsburgh, but across the nation. America would never again be Number One in heavy steel production, mostly as the result of foreign competition. Everybody in Pittsburgh — including football fans and players — knew it. Jack Lambert knew it because his career was in a steel town and because the place he was born was in the middle of what we call today "the rust belt."

He knew how generations of them had worked hard, how proud they'd been of their prestige as makers of the world's best quality steel. Wearing hard hats, safety glasses, heavy coveralls, and steel-toed shoes, the three or four who worked at the blast furnace knocked open the hinged doors of a hopper car. It sat on top of an inner-mill trestle, raw coke pouring out onto the ground below. Knocking the doors open didn't completely empty the car, so those "hot metal men" had to climb up the side ladder of the trestle, climb up the side of the hopper car, and jump inside with breaker bars and long-handled shovels. Their determination and muscle broke loose the rest of the coke and shoved it down the car's sloping floor, through the hinged doors. Now *those* guys were not "entertainers." Their work was hot and grimey in the summer, ice c-o-l-d in the winter. When winds whistled across the trestles, the wind-chill factor could hit 50° below.

Thinking about it, Lambert's face had tightened in serious thought. He knew all too well the contrast between pro-football as a career and one spent in the steel mills. He was fully aware of the huge sums pro players made. "The money we make," he bellowed at Tom Melody, "the good times we have — and these guys talk about pressure!"

When opportunity knocked, Lambert took advantage of it. He held down the middle of the Steeler defense a solid decade, and bogged down many an offense with his strong-arm tactics. "This is my 11th year, and I never expected to make it to ten," he admitted. "If I stay healthy, I can continue to have more good years."

Who would ever have thought that a <u>freak</u> injury would cost Jack his career? Too much heavy stress on a big toe and it was all over...an entire pro career whisked away in an instant. He would never run in those size-14 football shoes again. How does any football player deal with an injury? Is it just a matter of following a doctor's orders, going through treatment and a healing process then back to the field as if nothing had happened? Depending on the type of injury, a player can either make a comeback or face the fact that his career is over.

Many different kinds of injuries can sideline a player: concussions, shoulder injuries — knee, ankle, hip, finger and, yes, toe injuries. An athlete can sustain only so many of them until their cumulative effects end his career, in high school, college, or pro ball.

On the other hand, nobody likes to think much about the non-recovery kind of injury, the kind nobody can heal from, let alone play another second. No use recounting the stats. We see such injuries on the TV screen almost every week — in local high school, regional college, or professional games. That's the kind of hurt Lambert suffered when he acquired his final injury. "If it were any toe other than a big toe," Lambert mourned, "I could have it cut off and then go on playing football." Cut off a toe and continue? He can thank his lucky stars he's not consigned to a wheelchair the rest of his life!

Shortly before the Cleveland game in Three Rivers Stadium that year, Jack was put on the injured reserve list. Frustration set in as he watched the Steelers squeak by with a 23-20 win. Restless, he was out for the season — and finished forever as a player. His injury was as mysterious as Lambert himself. The hit that smashed his career came in the season opener against the Kansas City Chiefs. Linebacker Lambert planted his left foot on the synthetic turf, getting ready to make a tackle, putting too much force on the foot. As he pushed off to tackle the ball carrier, Blam! You can almost feel it, hear it yourself: *"Oh somebody come get me...I'm sick to my stomach."* Strain and pressure from the move broke his toe at the socket.

The rest is history. "Lambert hurt his toe when going after a tackle," Joe Gordon said. "He caught his foot in the turf and tore his toe loose. You know he was a very emotional player — on the sideline or in the game." When questioned about turf injuries, Gordon was less certain. "I'm not sure if synthetic turf causes more injuries than natural grass. I'm just not sure about it." Kenny Stabler had no doubts about it:

"Artificial turf was probably the worst thing ever created for football players. Ironically, it was supposed to be a godsend. Turf manufacturers claimed it would reduce knee injuries, but it has actually increased them. Turf does not give at all, so that a planted foot will not slide when you're hit — and then something has to go. Usually a knee or an ankle. I have seen players tear up knees and ankles just running and cutting on synthetic surfaces without being hit. And a number of top players like Lambert and Larry Csonka have had to retire early after suffering what is called 'turf toe,' where the foot gives to the surface, causing ligament and tissue damage."

More than 20 years ago, Bernie Parrish noted that helmets caused a lot of damage: "A helmet is a player's most dangerous weapon. Sixty percent of all serious football injuries are caused by blows from helmets." He also agreed with Stabler about artificial turf:

"Artificial turf may turn out to be the biggest bust ever if the records to date are any indication. The Houston Oilers had thirteen knee operations in 1970 and they play half their games on the Astroturf at the Astrodome. Infections from burns caused by sliding across the plastic grass were another new hazard."

And just think: that was 27 years ago!

"Today the abrasion-injury problem is most prominent with Astroturf," said Kent State University football trainer John Faulstick.

"There's no other difference in types of injuries when playing on grass or turf. Astroturf injuries are more severe than grass-related ones, but that depends on the quality of the turf. Turf has a life expectancy of four to seven years, and old turf is the problem."

So John disagrees with pro football players' ear...
that turf is bad, not good to play on. He admits freely th~~
ferences do exist.

> "But it's important to practice on turf and get
> accustomed to it, especially the week of a game that
> will be played on turf. The players learn to "cut
> and fall properly, reducing injuries. If you don't
> practice on turf before a turf game, you're in
> trouble."

K.S.U. has a grass home playing field (changing to artificial
turf), but an indoor turf field for practice when it's needed. Their
indoor facility is relatively new, six to seven years old. One year,
Kent State played on five Astroturf fields during out-of-town
games, and they were fortunate that those fields were relatively new.

> "Maybe some teams will wear extra padding
> on the elbows and knees when playing on astroturf.
> Teams that use extra padding are the ones who
> don't play a whole lot on turf to begin with."

Faulstick indicated that recent grass vs. turf injuries had
not been studied statistically — at least he'd seen no important
articles in the past five years in any of the sports medicine
magazines. He suggested that anyone interested should double-
check in the <u>Journal</u> of <u>Athletic</u> <u>Medicine</u> and <u>The</u> <u>Physician</u>
<u>and</u> <u>Sports</u> <u>Medicine</u> magazines.

"Weight training," he said, "does reduce football-related injuries. But attitude and talent are just as important, and a team
can win with these two attributes even if they don't weight-
train." He added that an average team could improve its level
of play simply by working on the weights. Remarkable statement. But talk to professional ball players and you'll hear an
even more remarkable angle: frequently, so they say, franchise
owners don't worry so much about player injuries as they do
about how pretty artificial turf looks on T.V. Owners are less
interested in player welfare than in the box office take and those
national T.V. contract fees. The lines stay so pretty and white
on that green artificial turf. They're easy to see. Teams don't

the mud and start looking like a can of tad-
robably has an opinion on one side or the other
hich is still being argued.

Bernie Parrish's comment about helmets, so let's
ne more quick note about football equipment. Ac-
cord... ?aulstick, the major equipment change over the years
has been in shoe construction. Shoes have been improved many
times over since Lambert received his toe injury. The "toe box"
(from the ball of the foot to the tips of the toes) is much <u>stiffer</u>,
giving much better toe support, and construction of the whole
shoe is of better quality.

In 1984, forced to stand on the sidelines all year, Lambert
was frustrated beyond description. He was unable to join his
team in a 9-7 record and their first-place finish in the AFC's
Central Division. When Pittsburgh made it to the AFC title
game, need-achiever Lambert felt totally helpless while Pittsburgh lost to the Miami Dolphins 45-28. "What if" Pittsburgh's
great linebacker had played in that game: you <u>know</u> he would
have made a difference. Cutting down opposing runners like
logs at the river, giving Pittsburgh a victory and another Super
Bowl trip, maybe even a Super Bowl win — one player can
make a big difference. Jack did throughout his whole career.

He ruminated, speculated, and pondered over the situation
during the off season. He drew an important, difficult conclusion about himself: he was at a crossroads in his life and would
need to take a new direction. So, in the summer of 1985, a July
10 news release stated that Jack Lambert wasn't going to report to training camp on July 19. The toe continued to cause
pain, and the defensive star never regained his push-off balance. Sportswriters had called him a "vampire" on defense who
blew smoke through his gapped teeth and sucked the blood and
energy out of enemy backfield players, but his histrionics were
over. No more high jinx or theatrics before each play.

On July 11, the day he officially announced his retirement
at Three Rivers Stadium, Lambert's stomach was full of but-
terflies. At his side stood Steeler Chairman Arthur Rooney, Sr.
Who in God's name would have thought a <u>toe</u> would end Jack

Lambert's football days? Maybe a gila monster out in the West. One of those critters can put an elephant out of action. "Last year was probably the most difficult in my life in regard to football," Lambert confessed. "It was the first time I didn't earn my paycheck. It was embarrassing to pick it up."

Team owner Art Rooney had thought that if Lambert relaxed for a while, he could play again. "But he couldn't believe a broken toe was going to stop him from playing." Rooney was from the old traditional football school. During the 1920's and 1930's, such injuries were unheard of, and if a player got hurt, he took it easy for a while. Or he just rubbed a little mud on the hurt and continued playing. Serious injuries happened then just as they do in modern-era football. Injury is the big culprit that prematurely ends a lot of pro careers.

"It's kind of embarrassing that Jack Lambert has to retire because of a toe. I've heard that for a year now," remarked Lambert. "You just don't realize how important that big toe is. It supports your whole body weight...It hurts [me] just to put on dress shoes."

In voicing his off-the-field opinions, Lambert had always been outspoken. To Jack, quarterbacks were sissified and should wear dresses — an opinion he voiced when rules were being made to protect quarterbacks. (How do you figure Lambert making such a statement? A former quarterback himself putting the noose of criticism around his own neck?)

Former Ohio State Head Coach Woody Hayes said it probably better than anyone regarding one's opinion: "Don't burn the bridges behind you," he said. "You might have to make a retreat."

Jack didn't burn any bridges in Pittsburgh. On the contrary, "bad news" Lambert found himself enshrined there, which gave him a sense of belonging. Art Rooney's prize collection of Steeler team pictures hangs at Three Rivers Stadium, one for each year he has owned the Steelers since 1933. Lambert is proud to know that he was the leading tackler in 10 of them. "This is a steel city. This is a football city," he said when he announced his retirement. "I think they always knew who was working hard out there."

After giving out farewells on retirement day, Jack didn't reveal any immediate plans — and said he didn't feel cheated out of playing more. "Right now, I'm not thinking beyond having a couple of beers," he said at the end of the press conference. "But as Joe Greene said when he retired, I want to thank you guys [the media] for letting me be Jack Lambert...I don't think a person who's played in nine Pro Bowls and four Super Bowls can feel cheated," he added. "My only regret is that it went too fast."

"Lambert made a total commitment to football and winning," Joe Gordon said, reminiscing. "I thought of him as a friend, someone to talk to easily, and a player who was popular with the rest of the team." When asked if he thought Pittsburgh could have won four Super Bowls without Lambert, Gordon declared, "There were a lot of great players on those Super Bowl Steelers teams. Without Lambert? I can't say whether we would have won or lost all four." Asked the same question a second time later, Gordon burst out loud, "Why are you still asking? He's a Hall of Famer!"

Twenty-four hours after Lambert retired, he became a sports analyst for a Pittsburgh TV station, accepting the job on a moment's notice. But he wasn't suited for it. "This is something that came about 'just like that'. " Lambert said. "I had lunch with a gentleman from the station Tuesday afternoon, and Friday I was here [working for the station]. I made a quick decision, then went home that night and thought, *What did I do?!*"

To be a good TV sports analyst, a person needs to be something of a John Madden or a Gifford, Dierdorf, Michaels or a Summerall — a personality with a gift for emphasizing or dramatizing parts of the game. Whatever it is, Jack didn't have it. Former teammates gave Lambert the raspberries, adding some unpleasant gestures. "I took a lot of abuse from them," Jack admitted. "Not that the media and I didn't get along. But I used to give them a hard time. We had an understanding...but now I'm one of them. I took it from everybody, Chuck Noll, too."

Jack had his own style of analyzing a game, explaining all

the details. If he didn't like something a team was doing, he openly criticized it. The opinionated former linebacker should have tried coaching instead. He would have reached greater heights, since he did like young people so well. At least he could have set the right example, not standing for mediocrity. That was something he spoke against as a player — and the players, coaches, and fans knew it.

Pro football in the mid-1980s was not the "animal act" some folks thought it was in its early days — when people didn't know anything about the pros. These days our men in the White House attend ball games — but back then? Red Grange liked to tell the story:

"...we went to the White House. ... December, 1925, a couple of weeks after I joined the Bears. We were playing an exhibition game with a team called the 'Washington All-Stars,' and it was the first time the Bears played in Washington, D.C. Senator McKinley of Illinois called George [Halas] and me and asked if we wanted to meet President Coolidge. The Senator sent his car to pick us up, and when we arrived, he introduced me to the President as 'Red Grange, who plays with the Bears.' Coolidge shook hands and said, 'Young man, I always liked animal acts.'"

Hard-nosed Lambert was neither an "animal act" nor a "Yes" man at the TV station, and his outspoken opinions caused difficulties for both station management and others directly involved in football. "A lot of people thought Jack's taking that job meant he was going to be a house man, but I knew better," Dan Rooney said. "When a guy like him takes a job like that, he's gonna do what he wants. He's gonna say things the players don't like. He's gonna say things the coaches don't like, and he's gonna say things I don't like."

At first Lambert looked at broadcasting as a chance to stay up with the game and follow some remaining teammates. "I thought it would be fun," he said. "I thought I would enjoy it. It gives me a chance to stay in touch with this football team. And

I think as long as there are guys on the team that I played with, I'm going to have a special interest." Only a few of Jack's teammates were left from the Super Bowl teams of the 1970s; time was growing short for them too.

Like the old cliche says, "All good things must come to an end." Good or not, Lambert's career as a sports analyst came to an end and he moved on to other things. Lambert was tired of public life. After so many years as a pro football star in the public eye, he wanted to rescind his celebrity status. He headed for the hills of Pennsylvania to establish a niche for privacy, the privacy he was always seeking and talking about as a player.

Explaining to Jim O'Brien (and quoted by Robert Johnson two years later), Lambert complained: "It got to the point where I couldn't even go to church without people turning around in the pew and looking at me. I can't go anywhere anymore because of the attention I get. Do you know I've even had people stop at the bottom of my driveway and just stare at my house?" We are reminded of Hollywood tours, especially the bus tour called "Homes of the Stars." Most of us don't understand it, but some people simply drive by and look at the homes of their stars.

When he retired, Lambert took with him his famous #58 jersey, memories of the crowd's cheers, and thoughts about the colors, highs, and lows of the game. He used that same football spirit, that same will to win, in building the retreat of his dreams. Jack concentrated on the renovation of an A-frame house that came with the purchase of the property. "It's something I'm doing in my spare time," Lambert boasted after admitting he had no carpentry skills. "It's still standing, and not from experience. I'm thinking about moving up there [permanently]. It should be done by the year 2000."

Lambert's new domain in the hills was an outdoorsman's haven. It sat in a wildlife moor unknown to many others, rather like his personal life was unknown. He always claimed his private life was nobody's business but his own—and that included his immediate family, details of his childhood and social life.

Fans had seen a "thespian" on the field, using all his antics to psych out players on opposing teams, but around Pittsburgh, fans came to know him better as an enigma. That's mostly how they think of him today. Why not? Imagine the 180° shift from one lifestyle to another, like going from noon to midnight, an about-face from celebrity to anonymity. "There is no question about that," Dan Rooney agreed. "He's not a hanger-on. He's no loafer. He gets on about his business...I can remember Super Bowls and Pro Bowls [when] Jack would often bring his father (John H. Lambert of Cleveland) with him to let him be a part of it. But once they left the locker room, it was very private. They would go off and do their own thing. He's a man's man."

On occasion, Lambert even told reporters, "Back off from my personal life." They swallowed it hook, line, and sinker. He really wasn't always anti-social, but there were times he just didn't want to talk about football. "I went to our 15-year high school reunion and saw some of those guys this past summer," he said. "I thought everybody was pretty much the same as when I left. They wanted to talk about professional football, and I wanted to talk about what was happening back there." About the only football enthusiast Lambert really liked to listen to was Steeler team owner Arthur Rooney, Sr.

According to Dan Rooney, "He enjoyed listening to my father. They'd sit down and talk about the old days of football. He was the guy my father said would fit in with Johnny Blood." For those who don't know, Johnny Blood (McNally) was a two-way back who played for the Green Bay Packers and the Steelers between 1925-1936. Johnny was inducted into the Pro Football Hall of Fame in 1963.

No lapse of 27 years occurred for Lambert between playing and professional recognition: On September 22, 1985, he was named to the All-NFL 25-Year Team. Lambert turned into (and remains today) a greatly admired celebrity who has "turned private."

Chapter XI
After Football

Despite 300 years of our attempts to exploit it, the Pennsylvania mountain area is still attractive: lakes, rivers, nearly two million acres of forests. It's a good place to relax, enjoy tranquillity and the good hunting and fishing. Especially the hunting. Every year Pennsylvania sells about 1,000,000 hunting licenses during whitetail deer season. A full-grown buck with a full antler rack (a 12-point buck) is one of nature's most elegant sights, whether you're a hunter or not.

Living in the cool beauty of those Pennsylvania mountains, enjoying every day in their natural peace, free to raise a family away from the big-city hassle: these are some of the things that money can't buy. Jack Lambert seems to value them above everything else. "The way I see it, it comes down to what is important," he said. "Is dying a billionaire important? Maybe to some people, but not to me...if I hustled for a dollar every day and lived a long life, I think I'd have regrets. But if I drop dead tomorrow, I'll die happy. I am doing exactly what I want."

Becoming a deputy Wildlife Conservation Officer (WCO) in Pennsylvania was exactly the right career alternative for Lambert after football. It's not really like work for him because he enjoys the animals and outdoors so very much. Unlike an everyday 9-to-5 job with heavy mental stress and tension, work in the big woods of the Keystone State assures the former Steeler peace of mind. It's a slower-paced occupation than football most of the year, depending on the season.

When deer hunting season is in full swing, things turn a

little hectic. Tracking down illegal hunters and wounded deer that drift off to die — deer season sometimes comes close to warfare with those 1,000,000 hunters tramping around the woods. There's always one fool in the group who will shoot at anything that moves — spelling danger, maybe costing some innocent hunter his life with a high-powered bullet meant for a deer. Most hunters are safe hunters and abide by the rules. "This is my busy season," said Lambert, "...deer season...I'm real busy. I'm out in the woods arresting bad guys: hunters without licenses, guys who aren't following the rules. And I'm picking up road kills...I like the job a lot, most of the time. But picking up deer that have been hit by semi-trucks, that's not my idea of fun."

Lambert made these statements in 1989, just before his first public appearance at Three Rivers Stadium since he'd retired in 1985. By his own choice, working as a game warden has kept Jack from public life, making him appear to be an "enigma" to lots of people in the Pittsburgh area. Even so, Barry Seth, Lambert's WCO supervisor has trouble keeping the former All-Pro Steeler under wraps. When he's on patrol duty, would-be hunters take nosy looks to try to figure out whether "that game warden" is really Lambert or not. The best story comes from a local hospital — involving a hunting-accident victim. After being interviewed, the victim wanted to know from the nurse if he was hallucinating during the interview. He had been so doped up that he couldn't believe who he saw standing in the hospital room. According to Seth, the man wasn't hallucinating and recognized Lambert as the deputy officer. In his field notes for documentation, Seth wrote, "No, his badge number is not No. 58." Seth never fully disclosed the field notes to anyone, citing Lambert's desire for privacy. Hey! Jack has it both ways: privacy at home and privacy at work.

Trying to get Lambert in the public eye is a difficult task. You need a wrecking bar to pry him loose from his hidey-hole in the hills. "I tried to get Lambert out to do something for the newspaper," said Steve Hubbard. Steve was a sportswriter for the <u>Pittsburgh Press</u> (now the Pittsburgh <u>Post-Gazette</u>). "He's just a private person who wishes to remain that way." Hubbard was the beat writer covering the Steelers, an assignment he covered for years, and knowing the mysterious former Steeler, at that time, on a first-name basis didn't help him bring Lambert out to speak in public.

Some time back, however, Jack knew some kind of sweet-talk. Soft-spoken Lambert must have whispered something appealing in her ear. She must have whispered some pretty special things in return: Jack and Lisa took each other in holy matrimony and headed for the hills. One thing that pleased Jack immensely: Art Rooney from the Pittsburgh Steelers was the first person to reply to the wedding invitation's R.S.V.P. Jack Ham answered quickly, too.

In the spring of 1988, they sold their home in Fox Chapel (Pittsburgh) and moved permanently to the farm in Armstrong County...a place that makes them both happy. Farm life was right up Jack's alley after having been raised on one. "I'm really happy where I'm at. There are animals everywhere at my place — ducks, a pen of quail, a parrot. The dog..." Willie The Dog is named after Willie Nelson, George The Parrot after George Jones. The animals are nice to have around, but they drive Lisa a little stir-crazy at times. All the livestock is hard to keep track of each day. Not for Jack, of course: they take him as far away from football as one could get.

"I drive my wife crazy with all the animals, but I'm living the life I always dreamed about. Our house isn't a 9-million dollar mansion, but it's comfortable and we like it... When I played football, I had two priorities. The first was to be the best I could be at the game. The second was to invest my money wisely and conservatively and not squander it so I could do what I wanted after I retired. I'm satisfied that I did both."

At the time he made those statements, Lambert was doing promotions for Hunter Station, a resort in Tionesta, Pennsylvania — great deer country (also great country for Anheuser-Busch) — and radio commercials for Budweiser, with sports announcer Myron Cope. "We sing in 'em. People are going to love it." Jack also was doing charity work at this time, but he kept his affiliations with the organizations anonymous: "I don't do those things because I want patted on the back."

The old need-achiever never wanted "patting on the back," but when it came time for induction (August 4, 1990) into the Pro Football Hall of Fame, he didn't fail to show up for the ceremony. The honor was bestowed to Lambert in his first year of eligibility (to be selected, a player must be retired at least five years). On January 27, 1990, officials counted the ballots and found Lambert had been chosen to be inducted. Dennis Fitzgerald, his coach from Kent State, made the presentation August 4, 1990. Fitzgerald's entire presentation is provided in Appendix A.

Jack's acceptance speech, acknowledging the award, is given in full in Appendix B. I'll include just one of its dramatic pictures:

> "...my mother, Joyce. When I was growing up [she was] my biggest fan and supporter. I can't ever remember playing in an athletic event that my mother did not attend. I can still see my mom late at night after a football game, scrubbing and soaking the grass stains out of my pretty white football pants. Mom thought it was very important that her son have the whitest pants on the field."

The Class of 1990 inducted into the Hall of Fame also included:

Teammate Franco Harris,

Former Dallas Cowboys coach Tom Landry,

Former Miami Dolphins quarterback Bob Griese,

Former San Francisco 49ers tackle Bob St. Clair,

Former Kansas City Chiefs' defensive tackle Buck Buchanan and

Former linebacker Ted Hendricks, who played for the Baltimore Colts, Green Bay Packers, Oakland and Los Angeles Raiders.

Both "Storks" made it together, the same year. What a happy coincidence.

But not Lynn Swann. How come? "When I heard about Lynn

Swann not making it, I thought about all the great players on our team who might not make it," Lambert said. "But there's no shame in that. Even if I didn't make it this year or in the future, that would have been fine because I'll always have my memories of playing for the Pittsburgh Steelers...no one can take [those memories] from me. They mean more to me than anything." Presumably they should for Swann, too...

How are players selected for such honors? Sometimes players are not sure just how the experts perceive them—or if Hall of Fame selection is fair or "just political." Hall of Fame inductees are not selected in chronological order like some people believe they should be. (A year or so ago, Don Maynard, Hall of Fame 1987, commented privately that many awards — like "outstanding Young Man of So-&-So" — are basically political, depending on what the awarders want the awardees to do in return.) Too true. So far as I know, though, football politics has nothing to do with being inducted into the Pro Football Hall of Fame.

Lambert declared, "You never really know how people perceive you as a football player...I guess some people think I'm one of the best who ever played the game, or else I wouldn't be in the Hall of Fame. That's very rewarding, a very gratifying feeling." One thing is for sure: you know how your teammates perceive you. Judging a comrade strictly on attitude and performance is one of the hardest kinds of evaluations, like conduct and proficiency marks in military service. In pro football, opponents even evaluate who they played against.

"Lambert was as good as any of the great linebackers against the run, but he was dramatically better than any of them against the pass," teammate Andy Russell recalled before Lambert's induction. "He called the defensive signals. He set the tone. He was intelligent, all business, a terrific leader."

Any way you cut the cake, Lambert made a number of contributions to the Steelers that led them to greatness. "Jack Lambert demanded a total effort from everybody in the organization," Steeler President Art Rooney said. "He took us to greatness. He was the symbol of our success in the 1970's... Of all the middle-linebackers — Ray Nitschke, Willie Lanier, Dick Butkus — what set Jack apart was his ability to defend against the pass."

How was the stage set for Lambert to make Hall of Fame induction? It had to begin somewhere. Was it luck or just being in the right place at the right time? Don't forget that many exceptional people never live up to their talents — and never receive applause for what they do achieve. "The stage was set at Kent State for Jack's Hall of Fame induction," said Gary Pinkel. "When Bobby Bender quit the team, he opened the door for Jack's Hall of Fame induction."

It's funny when a player says he didn't play to get into the Hall of Fame. It's something like a player who says he's not in the game for the money — and Biletnikoff put the quietus on that pompous old statement. Biletnikoff was right: "Anybody who says he doesn't do it for the money is full of nonsense." At least Franco Harris admitted that he wanted to make it.

What about Lambert? What was he doing on the pro football fields of the near past? He sure wasn't out there twiddling his thumbs. "I never played to get into the Hall of Fame," he insisted a few months before induction. "I just wanted to play the best I could for Mr. Rooney [the late Art Rooney, Sr.] and the Pittsburgh Steelers. I think I did that...I played the only way I could play. There was no plan to be a wild, crazy man out there. At my size, I had to be in the right frame of mind all the time."

But Jack does still get emotionally wound up about one game, and Franco Harris and other teammates share his regrets: it was the 1976 AFC championship game.

"The 1976...game against the Oakland Raiders," grumbled Lambert. "A lot of us felt we could have and should have won that game if Franco and Rocky [Blier] hadn't gotten hurt. If we had won it, then maybe there wouldn't be all this talk about the 49ers matching our four Super Bowls. We would have had five."

Was Lambert bothered by the fact that the 49ers might win their fourth Super Bowl? "I could care less," he insisted.

"No matter who you are, someone always comes along who is better. I can live with that."

So far nobody has proved to be better and, if they ever are, it won't be by much. As far as Lambert goes, he was recognized for his worthiness by induction into the Pro Football Hall of Fame. Harris and Lambert brought the total to six members of the golden era (1970s) Steelers to make it into the Hall of Fame. Joe Greene was chosen in 1987, Jack Ham in 1988, Terry Bradshaw and Mel Blount in 1989. A pretty tough bunch of hombres. There's always been talk about who was the "meanest" Steeler. It boiled down to two Steel Curtain heroes: Joe Greene and Jack Lambert. But Greene always relinquished full credit to the man stacked behind him on defense.

"He didn't like you if you had a different color jersey on," Greene said back in 1990.

"Heck, he didn't like half the guys with the same jersey on! ... Lambert was tremendously competitive. He didn't back down against anybody. Whether it meant stepping over people or running through people, he did it. I don't know if I can call him mean. He's just a tough, ferocious player.

"He took a tremendous beating. Every time Lambert took on a guard, he was probably outweighed by 50 pounds minimum. That takes its toll. There were many times Jack was beat up and banged up and his actions spoke louder than his words. Lambert shows up the entire week in the whirlpool, ice pads on his ribs and knees and ankles, you think each step will be his last, but when he shows up on Sunday, not one of us could not show up because of little bruises or hangnails."

All during his career, Lambert played with pain, and his total concentration blocked it out. It took an act of courage each time he ran onto the field. If you want to be great, you've got to play with pain, and most players do at one time or another. There's no half-steppin' permitted. It's a "full-go" effort all the time.

"His really big contribution was his focusing power, his ability to be one-dimensional," Chuck Noll said before Jack's trip to Canton. "His attitude was *let's get this done*. Let's focus." He was an emotional leader. His ability to focus was over and above his physical ability."

What did Lambert think about his Hall of Fame induction? In one final statement, he said, "I played the only way I knew how. I played aggressively. I had to. I had to be in the right frame of mind. I played that way in high school, I played that way in college. That's how I got into the pros..."

And into the Hall of Fame.

By the time this book goes to press, another former Pittsburgh Steeler will be happy, too. Chuck Noll, who guided the Lambert-led teams to four Super Bowl championships was in the Class of 1993 inductees into the Pro Football Hall of Fame. Pretty soon the Steelers may need their own wing in Canton to house all the players from their club enshrined there.

EPILOGUE

You and I have gone nearly as far as we can go in our look at the career of an outstanding football player. It's time to try to gain some perspective. As Lambert himself would say, "Let's get this done." Fans will speculate about the motivation, the fundamental drive, behind the nationally acclaimed hero we know as Jack Lambert, and we really must contribute what we can to understanding.

Nearly all the people I've spoken to, all who knew him during his football career and before, eventually admit they don't really know him. Even as a teenager, his classmates spoke of the "distance" he kept between himself and the rest of the crowd. His relative, Louise Harper, spoke of the "distance" he drew away from his family. Nobody has been able to penetrate that to understand the intense motivation, the desire—all right, the compulsion—driving this complex Hall of Famer to his heights of achievement. Borrowing the title from Bud Schulberg's <u>What Makes Sammy Run</u>?, everybody wonders <u>What Made Jack Lambert Run</u>? What still "makes him tick"?

One cold, light snowy February evening, John Pennell talked with me about his close friend, Jack Lambert. John's voice is Midwestern with a slow twang. That night he spoke clearly, precisely, backing up when he wanted to emphasize a point. Pennell lives alone in a red brick duplex — its front flanked by evergreen shrubs — in Streetsboro, Ohio. He's a carpenter, and his work papers and tools were scattered around the living area. Big John is 6-ft. tall, fluctuating between 230 and 240 lbs. — size 52 jacket — and he wears heavy wire-rimmed glasses that won't break easy. The night we talked, John was sitting on the couch watching TV with no sound, keeping the mute button suppressed.

"Jack never was a spot-light person," he said. "Jack just wanted to prove to all his coaches and everyone that he could do it. It was because of the negative feedback he got all his life — not being big enough, not being fast enough or heavy enough."

Years ago another Ohio native, James Wright, created the image of a Friday night high school football game. In his poem "Autumn Begins In Martin's Ferry, Ohio," Wright spoke of the night watchman and the hot metal men working at the blast furnace of a steel mill. He saw them as fathers "dreaming of heroes," suggesting that their sons try to fulfill their fathers' dreams by becoming high school football heroes. That may be true of a lot of players — from grade school right up through the pro's. Apparently it's not true of Jack Lambert.

He truly admired and enjoyed sharing ideas with two influential older men: the aging monk, Father Raymond at the St. Vincent summer training camps, and Dan Rooney's father — owner of the Steelers. But they certainly were not what the pop-psychologists would call "father substitutes." We know that, after all the horseplay and high jinks of the locker room, he was a serious student of literature and philosophy — nose in a book, reading, learning, gaining understanding — while teammates were out spending their cash on the glitz and glitter of big-time sports. We know he had some excellent coaches, that he listened and paid attention to what they said. His Uncle Larry Marek probably said it better than anybody: Lambert was simply more *mature* than most of his classmates.

Let me suggest that everybody stop looking for "hidden meanings," that we all take the man at his word and pay attention to what <u>he</u> said motivated him. I am convinced that the celebrity we know as Jack Lambert believed what his parents, teachers, and coaches told him when he was a little kid — that if he tried hard enough, if he really did his very best, he could achieve what he wanted to. Nobody ever put out more effort.

Why wouldn't he consent to interviews for this book? How many of us would like for strangers to go poking around in the past to find out what we've done? Say we were interested in politics or public office. Nobody wants the public turning a spotlight on his private life. Maybe the man simply wants to be left alone.

Lambert has said it over and over and over again, so we might as well listen: two things have been important to him—playing football the very best he could, and saving his money for the future. He's done both. It seems he understands his own childhood and the effects it had on him.

From his public statements we know that he's always known his personal limitations. He knew what it would take to overcome those limitations in order to achieve his goals.

I believe he's a religious man but not a church-goer —not a saint, but a man of principle. As he has expressed them, his principles pertain to all walks of life: (1) do whatever you do with your very best effort and you can reach your goal; (2) if for some reason you fail, that's all right. Because there will always be somebody "better" and YOU will know you did your best. What other people think doesn't matter. I suspect that Jack Lambert is probably living the American dream.

APPENDIX "A"

PRESENTATION SPEECH
TO PRO FOOTBALL HALL OF FAME
AUGUST 4, 1990

—BY DENNIS FITZGERALD

"Mr. Commissioner, Chairman Stu, presenters and inductees and football people of all ranks and stations, my particular chore here today is a very easy one because I think my inductee fits this institution just like air to a football. Robert Service, the great poet of the Yukon, wrote [the] words, "There is a race of men that don't fit in," and I think if he were in Stark County today I think he might change his words looking at these inductees because there is a race of men that fit right in.

"Jack Lambert was born in neighboring Portage County right up the road, attending Crestwood High School, a quarterback no less, went to Kent State University and there from defensive end to middle-linebacker, where his football honors started to grow. He was drafted in 1974 in the second round by the Pittsburgh Steelers. His success was immediate. In his first year he was defensive rookie of the year; he was also an important contributor to the first of four Super Bowls that Pittsburgh was to obtain. He proceeded to add nine consecutive pro bowl appearances — a record for NFL linebackers. In 1976 and 1979, he was voted the NFL's defensive player of the year. He had 28 career regular season interceptions, had 1,441 tackles—and that is a _lot_ of contact.

"He had complete mastery of his position and he was a great cover linebacker, especially as middle-linebackers run. But these things are not as important as what all of you up there identify with Jack Lambert. He was one intense, tough football player. When he called a defense in a huddle there were 10 other defensive players [who] knew blasted well that defense would work. Jack Lambert was exciting to watch, was a joy to coach—but he was a lousy buck-euchre player. He is now retired to the hills of Pennsylvania where he and his lovely wife, Lisa, are raising two quarterbacks in dresses.

"Ladies and gentlemen, I give you #58 of the Pittsburgh Steelers, the wheel behind the Steel Curtain: Jack Lambert."

APPENDIX "B"

ACCEPTANCE SPEECH
TO PRO FOOTBALL HALL OF FAME
AUGUST 4, 1990

—BY JACK LAMBERT

"Thank you, thank you very much. Thank you, let's get this done.

"It goes without saying that to be inducted in the Pro Football Hall of Fame is the ultimate honor that a football player can receive. It should also go without saying that one does not come to stand on these steps without the guidance, the direction, and the support of others.

"In the short time that I am allotted today, I would like to start with my mother, Joyce. When I was growing up [she was] my biggest fan and supporter. I can't ever remember playing in an athletic event that my mother did not attend. I can still see my mom late at night after a football game, scrubbing and soaking the grass stains out of my pretty white football pants. Mom thought it was very important that her son have the whitest pants on the field. Thank you, Mom, for all those special little things you did for me that I will never forget.

"My father, Jack...I get my athletic ability and temperament from my father's side of the family. Most of the time we spent together was throwing the baseball back and forth or playing tackle football. Back before the days of NFL Properties, my dad had enjoyed buying football helmets and painting them the colors of the NFL teams. The helmet he chose to paint for his son at that time was the Pittsburgh Steeler helmet. Thank you, Dad.

"Looking back to my days of playing football, my teammates and I won a championship in high school, college, and the pros. In order to do that you must have exceptional talent. But you must also have great coaching. Throughout my entire football career, I was truly blessed with that. My high school head coach was Gerry Meyers. I went up to ask Coach Myers if I could wear the #00. He said, 'Jack, that is a very special number, if you want 00 you have to be a very special player.' And then he asked me if I had what it took, and I couldn't answer that then, but I think I've answered that today. Thank you, Coach Myers.

"My head coach in college was Don James, the only Kent State coach to win a Mid-American championship, and his record and the

success he is still enjoying today out in Washington speaks for itself. Thank you, Coach James. And, of course, Chuck Noll, who will one day be standing here on these very same steps to join Coach Landry and so many great coaches before him.

"And with all these fine head coaches, there was always one very special assistant coach that for some reason or other took me under his wing and always, always spent the extra time with me that was needed. In high school it was Dean Ishieda; Dean is here today. Thank you for coming, Dean. In college it was Dennis Fitzgerald and in the pros it was Bob Widenhofer who is now with the Detroit Lions. I could have chosen any one of these men to be my presenter today, because they were all so instrumental in my success. But I chose Coach Fitzgerald because I thought he, more than anyone else, taught me the techniques and the fundamentals I used throughout college and professional football. But maybe more importantly he took a raw talent and a raw toughness in me and refined it into a mental discipline—a discipline that is necessary to excel. Thank you, Coach Fitzgerald.

"I would also like to thank the NFL, an organization that enabled me to realize a boyhood dream, an organization that afforded me an opportunity to travel to Europe and Southeast Asia on USO tours with my good friend Billy Granholm, and an organization that has given to me many cherished memories and friendships. On the day I retired from pro ball, I made this statements; 'There is not an owner, or a team, or a coaching staff, or a people in a city that I would rather have played for in the entire world.' The kindness that Arthur J. Rooney and his family have shown me — and the kindness the people of Pittsburgh have shown me over the years — are kindnesses that I can never repay. Five years later, I appreciate and stand by those words even more.

"How fortunate I was to play for Art Rooney and his family. How fortunate to be associated with the entire organization. The front office people, the coaching staff, the medical staff — Dr. Best, Dr. Huber, Dr. Steele, the trainers headed by Ralph Berlin and Ralph Miley — who did their best to stitch me up and piece me together for 11 years. And the most important people in the organization: the locker room and equipment men, Jackie Hart, Tony Parisi, Rodgers Freyvogel, Frankie and Mike.

"I was so fortunate to have played on some of the greatest teams of all time and arguably the greatest defense ever assembled. And finally, how fortunate I was to play for the Pittsburgh fans...a proud

and hard-working people who love their football and their players. If I could start my life all over again, I would be a professional football player and you blasted well better believe I would be a Pittsburgh Steeler!

"To my family, to my friends, to all my teammates from Crestwood and Kent State, to all of you fans out there who will never be in any Hall of Fame, at the risk of sounding a bit pretentious I give this day to you. This is your day and this is your Hall of Fame. I would like my wife, Lisa, and my daughters to stand. There, Ladies and Gentlemen, is my Hall of Fame. Thank you. God bless."

APPENDIX "C"
RESOURCES CONSULTED

Alexander, Elton. "Lambert Was All Business On and Off the Field." September 5, 1985.

Arnold, Lynn. "Now Lambert Stadium," Record Courier. October 10, 1980. p. 1-14.

Augusta, Bob. "Old Master Rates Lambert No. 1," Cleveland Press. September 17, 1976.

Bissinger, H.G. Friday Night Lights: A Town, a Team, and a Dream. Addison-Wesley Publishing Company, Inc. New York, N.Y. 1990, p. 284.

Carnicelli, Joe. "Lambert Contented...." Kent Record-Courier, January 5, 1976, p. 12.

Cohen, Richard M., David S. Neft, Jordan A. Deutsch, and Ed Stone. "The Season," Pro Football Weekly's Football Almanac. New York - San Diego, 1979-1980. p. 26.

Cook, Ron. "Lambert Is Keeping Promise... Privately," The Pittsburgh Press. February 7, 1988. p. D1, D8.

_____. Pittsburgh Post-Gazette. February 12, 1989.

_____. "Lambert To Join Award Ceremony for Blount," Pittsburgh Post-Gazette. December 2, 1989.

Devault, Harry. "A Decade After Lambert, Hedderly," Record Courier, p.3-14, September 28, 1982.

Dulac, Gerry. "Lambert's Fame Built on Fierce Dedication," The Pittsburgh Press. January 28, 1990.

"Enshrinement Ceremonies" (mimec, partial copy) 1990 PRO FOOTBALL HALL OF FAME August 4, 1990. 2121 George Halas Drive N.W., Canton, Ohio 44708.

_____. "Harris, Lambert Hall of Fame Bound," Pittsburgh Post-Gazette. January 29, 1990.

Felser, Larry. "NFL Roundup: American Conference," Street and Smith's - Official Yearbook - Pro Football. 1979.

_____. "Pro Football: Too Rough," Pro Football Official Yearbook. Street and Smith, 1979.

Flynn, George L., ed. Red Smith, Intro. Vince Lombardi on Football. Galahad Books. New York, NY, 1973.

Gelman, Steve. Pro Football Heroes: Oh, No, Say It's Not You. Scholastic Book Service, New York. 1968.

Hapanowicz, Steve. "Lambert — Study in Intensity," Cleveland Plain Dealer, Friday, October 20, 1972.

Hayes, Woody. Former Ohio State University Head Coach. (Well-known quotation after his release.)

Heaton, Chuck. "Lambert Holds His Own," Cleveland Plain Dealer.

December 1, 1976; p. D-3.

_____. "Jack Lambert Says Goodbye," Cleveland Plain Dealer. July 12, 1985.

"Veteran Lambert Remains Heart of Team's Defense," Cleveland Plain Dealer, July/August 1983.

Higdon, Hal. Inside Pro Football. Grosset & Dunlap, New York: 1968.

Howard, Johnette. "Lion Hearted," Sport Magazine. September, 1992.

Huttner, Richard. Super Bowl Highlights. Weekly Reader Books: Middletown, CT. 1981.

Jones, Robert F. "A Living Legend Called Mean Smilin' Jack," 1976. K.S.U. Sports Information Department.

Klein, Dave. The Pro Football Mystique. New American Library, New York. 1978.

KSU Sports Information Department: list of quotes from Dennis Fitzgerald.

Lebovitz, Hal. "Prevent Defense, Prevented A Win," Cleveland Plain Dealer. Secton C, p. 1.

Livingston, Pat. "Lambert No Lamb in Steeler Middle Pasture," The Sporting News. September 11, 1976.

Lombardi, Vince. Quote from newspaper clipping. No title, n.d.

Lustig, Dennis. "Rookie Jack Lambert Stars in Violent World." Sports Weekender, the Cleveland Plain Dealer, December 28, 1974, Section 6C.

Madden, John with Dave Anderson. One Knee Equals Two Feet. Jove Books, New York. 1986.

Madden, John. Hey, Wait A Minute. Villard Books (Random House), New York, NY., 1984.

Melody, Tom. "Time Growing Short For Lambert," Akron Beacon Journal, August 1983, p. B1, B3.

_____. "Part-time Coach, Full-time Player," Akron Beacon Journal. June 25, 1984; p. D1-D-5

"Unable to Toe the Line Any Longer," Akron Beacon Journal. December 13, 1984; p. Fl.

Meyer, Ed. "Same Old Jack," Akron Beacon Journal. December 31, 1982, p. D1, D7.

Mysienski, Skip and Linda Kay, "Odds and Ins," Chicago Tribune. Section #4, p. 14. September 17, 1984.

"Multi-Year Contract Ends Holdout," Akron Beacon Journal. August 31, 1977; p. D-2.

Nack, Bill. "Linebacker Image Bugs Lambert," Akron Beacon Journal. September 24, 1976; p. C-S.

Nash, Bruce and Allan Zullo. The Football Hall of Shame. Pocket Books: New York, 1986.

Neft, David S., Richard M. Cohen, and Jordan A. Deutsch. The Sports Encyclopedia: Pro Football. Grosset and Dunlap. New York, NY. 1978.

New York (UPI). "Lambert, Chambers Gain Defensive Honors." 1976. K.S.U. Sports Information Department.

Phillips, Bum and Ray Buck. He Ain't No Bum. A Signet Book. New York, NY., 1980.

Pro Football Hall of Fame All-Time Greats: Class of 1990. Jack Lambert, Inductee. News release, 1990.

Rappoport, Leon. Personality Development: The Chronology of Experience. Scott, Foresman and Co. Illinois, 1972. Reference to Glueck and Glueck, 1950.

Resciniti, Angelo G. Super Bowl Victories. Willowisp Press, Inc. 401 E. Wilson Bridge Road, Worthington, Ohio. 1985.

Rohrer, Persh. "Last-second Score Dooms -Browns," Record Courier. November 17, 1980.

Sachs, Adam. "Decade of Fire: Jack Lambert, the Steel Curtain's Last Survivor, still Plays with Intensity." 1984.

San Diego (AP). "Pittsburgh wins title after waiting 40 years," Akron Beacon Journal. Dec. 18, 1972.

Scholl, Bill. "Lambert Starts For Steelers," 1974.

_____. "But For the Bad Guys." 1974.

Shippy, Dick. "Beyond A Doubt," Akron Beacon Journal, p. C-6, January 28, 1990.

Smith, Don. "Jack Lambert, 1990 Enshrines," Pro Football Hall of Fame (news release). April 1, 1990.

Stabler, Ken and Berry Stainback. Snake. Charter Books, New York. 1986.

"TD Club To Honor Lambert," Cleveland Plain Dealer. January 12, 1977. K.S.U. Sports Information Department.

UPI. Record Courier. October 13, 1980.

Walsh, Bill and Glenn Dickey. Building A Champion. St. Martin's Paperbacks (SMP). New York, NY: 1990.

Weir, Tom. "Steelers' Lambert: Last of Dying Breed Loses his Bite," U.S.A. Today. July 12, 1985.

Whittingham, Richard. The Meat Market: The Inside Story of the NFL Draft. MacMillan Publishing Co., New York. 1992. p.114.

Whittingham, Richard. The Fireside Book of Pro Football. Simon and Schuster. New York, 1989.

TOUGH AS STEEL